# COLOSSIANS
# & PHILEMON
# FOR YOU

# MARK MEYNELL

# COLOSSIANS & PHILEMON FOR YOU

**Colossians & Philemon For You**
© Mark Meynell/The Good Book Company, 2018

Published by:
The Good Book Company

Tel (UK): 0333 123 0880
Tel (US): 866 244 2165
Email (US): info@thegoodbook.com
Email (UK): info@thegoodbook.co.uk

**Websites:**

North America: www.thegoodbook.com
UK: www.thegoodbook.co.uk
Australia: www.thegoodbook.com.au
New Zealand: www.thegoodbook.co.nz

(Hardcover) ISBN: 9781784983000
(Paperback) ISBN: 9781784982935
(ebook) ISBN: 9781784983017

Design by André Parker

Printed in India

# CONTENTS

To my dear *Hasat* sisters and brothers
scattered across Turkey

# SERIES PREFACE

Each volume of the *God's Word For You* series takes you to the heart of a book of the Bible, and applies its truths to your heart.

The central aim of each title is to be:

- Bible centred
- Christ glorifying
- Relevantly applied
- Easily readable

You can use *Colossians & Philemon For You:*

**To read.** You can simply read from cover to cover, as a book that explains and explores the themes, encouragements and challenges of this part of Scripture.

**To feed.** You can work through this book as part of your own personal regular devotions, or use it alongside a sermon or Bible-study series at your church. Each chapter is divided into two (or occasionally three) shorter sections, with questions for reflection at the end of each.

**To lead.** You can use this as a resource to help you teach God's word to others, both in small-group and whole-church settings. You'll find tricky verses or concepts explained using ordinary language, and helpful themes and illustrations along with suggested applications.

These books are not commentaries. They assume no understanding of the original Bible languages, nor a high level of biblical knowledge. Verse references are marked in **bold** so that you can refer to them easily. Any words that are used rarely or differently in everyday language outside the church are marked in grey when they first appear, and are explained in a glossary towards the back. There, you'll also find details of resources you can use alongside this one, in both personal and church life.

Our prayer is that as you read, you'll be struck not by the contents of this book, but by the book it's helping you open up; and that you'll praise not the author of this book, but the One he is pointing you to.

*Carl Laferton, Series Editor*

**Bible translations used:**

- NIV: New International Version (2011 edition). This is the version being quoted unless otherwise stated.

- ESV: English Standard Version.

# INTRODUCTION TO COLOSSIANS AND PHILEMON

Visit Colossae today, and there is nothing to see.

Despite being only a brief but stunning drive down Turkey's Lycus Valley from the breathtaking sites of Laodicea and Hierapolis, all that remains is a large hill with the odd block of masonry jutting out on one side. The city was destroyed by a devastating earthquake that struck the valley in around AD 60. Unlike its two illustrious neighbours, Colossae was never rebuilt, presumably because the risk of more seismic activity was great. When I visited recently, I was quite disappointed, to say the least. But this is the probable reason why the Colossian church was not included in Jesus's letters to the seven churches of Revelation 2 – 3. When John the **apostle***** was exiled on the island of Patmos, it no longer existed.

So, we could say that the only legacy to us of this once thriving city is Paul's letter to the Colossian Christians. That is quite strange once you appreciate that, to the best of our knowledge, Paul never actually went there. But that never diminished the letter's impact, because Paul knew the world they lived in. For, as inhabitants of the Roman province of Asia, they all belonged to one of history's greatest empires: they were Roman subjects in Caesar's world.

Except that wasn't the whole story. They were also Christ-followers living in Christ's world. Despite having never met the Colossians, and despite the separation forced by his languishing in prison, Paul is insistent on that fact. He was well aware of how subversive and dangerous this message was.

---

* Words in **grey** are defined in the Glossary (page 200).

It is not usually until it gets pointed out that modern readers realise just how bold this letter to the Colossians really is. Paul is shockingly, dangerously politically incorrect. He is writing to people that he has never met nor is likely to meet (unless he could fulfil the hopes expressed in Philemon 22). He only has the report of their mutual friend Epaphras to go on (see Colossians 1:7). But still, he has the audacity to write to them about their lives and faith, to instruct and even to challenge them. But far more courageous is his determination to speak of cosmic and eternal realities in universal terms. He sees the world in black and white (with everyone split between the dominion of darkness and the kingdom of light), and towering over all stands Jesus Christ. Whatever Christ has said or achieved is automatically true for every person at every time in every place. There are no exceptions. He is the universal king. This is what gives Paul such confidence in applying Christian truths to these strangers. This is what made him courageous in the face of martyrdom. But he knew how important it was to be crystal clear for these young believers because so much was stacked up against them.

Rome's propaganda was straightforward. It convinced Roman sub-

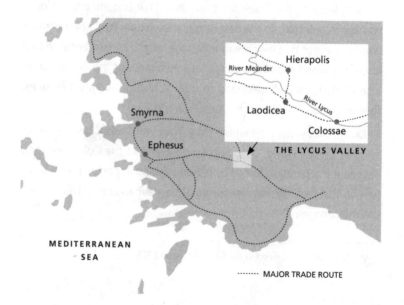

jects that they were far better off supporting the empire because it was the only system that could guarantee security in an uncertain world. The Latin word *pax* (meaning "peace") could be seen everywhere—on temple walls, on city gates, on official documents. As one historian wrote, adopting the guise of a Roman citizen:

> "Coins have Pax, the goddess of peace, on one side, and weapons on the other. Our gateways depict the emperor's victories over his enemies. This is peace by the blood of the sword."
>
> (*Colossians Remixed*, page 52)

Even in the earliest days of the empire, adoration of the emperor was actively encouraged. Take the poet Horace, who lived during the reign of the first Caesar, Augustus. His **sycophantic** verses declared that the emperor had "brought back fertile crops to the fields" and "wiped away our sins and revived the ancient virtues" (*Colossians Remixed*, page 54). That's quite the achievement!

Peace. Provision. Forgiveness.

These are basic human needs. Yet who could truly be relied upon to deliver? Paul knew that Caesar never could. And he was prepared to risk everything to say so. In fact, he knew he would pay the ultimate price for proclaiming it. But both the truth and glory of the alternative made it all worthwhile.

For it is God's Christ (and it emphatically was not Rome's Caesar) who holds everything together in ultimate peace and security. Even when it did not always seem or feel like it.

Colossians is about the universe's deep reality, despite appearances to the contrary. It is **worldview**-shaping, mind-expanding and game-changing. The stronger our grasp of its message, the greater our open-mouthed astonishment will become. If our first response to the teaching of this letter is not "Wow!" we are missing something. But we can't stay open-mouthed without falling to our knees. For if Jesus really is the cosmic Lord, then how can we not dedicate every fibre of our being to him and his service?

Whenever astronauts go into orbit for the first time, they all apparently experience the same sensation: the so-called "overview effect". Being able to see the whole of planet Earth at a glance changes everything: the fragility of life on this "pale blue dot" is palpable; national boundaries no longer seem that significant; petty concerns are dissolved by a galactic perspective. It is said to be truly overwhelming. Only a precious few have had this privilege. But all who read and absorb Colossians can gain something even more remarkable: God's overview effect.

When we see clearly that King Jesus is Lord of everything—nothing can ever be the same again.

# 1. A NEW FRIENDSHIP

Paul is clear from the outset where his allegiances lie. Sharing his opening greeting with his trusted right-hand man, Timothy, he describes himself as "an apostle of Christ Jesus by the will of God" (**v 1**)*. He is Christ's man, not Caesar's man, mandated by the Lord himself as one of his apostles, responsible for laying the foundations for God's new kingdom people. But if this seems a little formal, any distance is removed by what he, Timothy, and the Colossians have in common. He writes to them as "God's holy people in Colossae, the faithful brothers and sisters in Christ" (**v 2**), just as Timothy is "our brother" (**v 1**). These are no empty words: they form the bonds that connect them—and us—across time, distance and culture.

Contrary to a common misunderstanding, being described as "holy" is not a moral judgment—it is not a matter of how high one has reached on some sort of righteousness ladder. After all, Paul had never met these Christians, so how could he possibly make such an assessment? Instead, his point is that their holiness is a statement of fact: a declaration of what God has done in and for these believers. Their holiness and faithfulness to Christ are the direct results of their being "in Christ" (a central theme of Colossians). This is what binds them all together, and is the foundation of everything, Paul will write.

Similarly, "Grace and peace to you from God our Father" (**v 2**) is

---

* All Colossians and Philemon verse references being looked at in each chapter are in **bold**.

no hollow **platitude**. Those two words are actually key to what sets Christ's cosmic rule apart from that of anyone else (Caesar included). For who else can offer to every person on earth the wonders of God's undeserved forgiveness and mercy? Who else can restore us (and the entire creation) to everything we were created to be? This is real peace. Even though he is writing in Greek, Paul would have been completely familiar with the Hebrew concept of "*shalom*", a word which does not translate easily into either Greek or English. It is not simply the absence of hostilities; it is the settled and contented wholeness and flourishing that inevitably result from God's work in his world. It is ultimately the perfect peace that once existed in the Garden of Eden: a peace which the world cannot fathom, and which only originates from Christ himself (see John 14:27). It is the kind of peace that casts out all fear and anxiety.

So Paul's greeting is genuinely weighty and thrilling—and a tiny foretaste of the wonders to come.

## Deep gratitude

The pleasure Paul has in writing this letter comes from everything he has heard about his Colossian sisters and brothers. The church had been planted a few years previously by Epaphras (see Colossians **1:7**), a local who had returned home after his conversion (see 4:12-13). Epaphras was clearly a trusted member of Paul's team ("a faithful minister of Christ on our behalf" 1:7). So, when he passes on news of the Colossians' discipleship, Paul is thrilled (**v 3**). With so much in Roman culture stacked against the possibility of this happening, it was a terrific encouragement.

Paul's gratitude to God is prompted by various elements.

## "Your faith in Christ Jesus"

Personal confidence and trust in Christ (**v 4**) is of course the essential component for the Christian—both at the start of the disciple's journey and for the rest of life. But Paul was not simply excited because new converts had been added to their numbers. He knew how costly this was, how countercultural it was at a time when Christianity was such a new phenomenon in the region. For not only were the Colossians making a positive statement by accepting Jesus; they were also rejecting all the other gods and ideologies on offer.

But theirs was no mere intellectual excitement about a novel idea or religious fad.

## "The love that you have for all God's people"

Their new allegiance inspired a new service to their new brothers and sisters in Christ. As he says at the end of the paragraph, this is "love in the Spirit" (**v 8**). This love is not a matter of hollow sentimentality but effort and costly commitment. It is about identifying and meeting the needs of those around them. More than that, it is love that is indiscriminate—it is "for all God's people", or as the ESV translates it more accurately "for all the saints". It is an

> A saint is ... someone that God has declared holy and forgiven and therefore part of God's people.

immediate repetition of the word translated in **verse 2** as "God's holy people". A saint is a technical term in the Bible, someone that God has declared holy and forgiven, and therefore part of God's people. This fact alone was the radical incentive for the Colossians' love for others. Epaphras had clearly told Paul that there was no favouritism among them. Instead, there was ample evidence of practical love pouring out for all those who had need—just as had happened when the Jerusalem church began a few years before (see Acts 4:32-35). Perhaps this indiscriminate love is the most compelling aspect of Epaphras' report. Love for those who are different from us (be they Christian or not) is so counter to human nature that it surely points to this being the Holy Spirit's work. How else would it really come about?

The logic of how Paul orders the so-called Christian's trinity of faith, love and hope is surprising. We might expect to find love for others and hope of heaven to derive from trusting Christ. But here, the lynchpin for faith and love is in fact hope.

## "Hope stored up for you in heaven"

The Colossians have confidence about their future (Colossians **1:5**) because of what is prepared and ready for them—in God's eternal presence. Epaphras has seen how future-focused they are—but as their practical love proves, it is not a focus that tries to ignore present trials and challenges. It is simply that their confidence gives them what they need to persevere through them (**v 7-8**).

The reason believers can endure through hardship is that Christian hope is emphatically not wishful thinking. They are not idly holding out for a kind of spiritual lottery jackpot. Their hope does not depend on luck. Instead, hope's core is a promise—which is why Paul equates hope with the message he and countless others like Epaphras proclaim. "The hope … you have already heard in the true message of the gospel that has come to you" (**v 5-6**). God's promises in Christ are what make this news good: that is because they are all about that grace we have already touched on. The Colossian Christians understood it (**v 6**) and knew it to be true. That is why they hoped for it.

They were not the only ones. People were embracing this gospel "in the whole world", and this was "bearing fruit and growing" in lives of Christian love and faith. That is all evidence of God's surprising and inspiring work. No wonder Paul is thrilled and grateful.

So even though Paul has never met them, these believers from Colossae are very dear to him. Their conversion fills him with God-filled joy. Their lives exhibit precisely the qualities we should always expect in new believers:

- faith in Christ

- love for all God's people

- hope for heaven

This paragraph raises the obvious question of how someone might report on our own Christian walk. What evidence is there that we are "saints"; holy people?

That is, of course, a trick question! It is not an invitation to calculate how many holiness points we might have accumulated. Even less is it an invitation to discern someone else's spiritual achievements. Instead, it is a matter of examining the reality of the faith and love springing from our hope.

## Questions for reflection

1. Faith, hope and love: In what ways can our hope for heaven motivate both our love and our faith now (v 5)? Which of these three areas of Christian believing and living do you think you are weakest on? Why might that be?

2. Think about your own conversion to Christ. How do you usually describe it? How might you describe it differently in the way that Paul does in verses 6-8?

3. Why is genuine faith never just believing things are true—that is, intellectual assent? What else is required to make it real?

## PART TWO

### A new commitment

If you want to discover a person's real priorities, there are two key questions to ask: what do you spend most money on, and what do you most often pray for yourself and others? To turn it around the other way, let me ask you this question: if somebody had access to your bank statements and prayer lists, what would they conclude? Who or what is the focus of your life from this evidence?

We would have to work quite hard to learn much about Paul's spending habits (though some hints can be found in his letters). But he has left us a great deal to go on to understand his prayer priorities. It is telling that as soon as Epaphras gives him news of these Colossian brothers and sisters, he gets straight down to work—in prayer (**v 9**). That serves them even more effectively than visiting them in person.

"For this reason, since the day we heard about you, we have not stopped praying for you."

So, what does he commit to praying for?

### 1. From knowledge of God to worthiness for God

It may seem bizarre and hard to imagine, but some Christians claim to find **theology** dull and irrelevant. Yet, how can delving into the depths of who God is and what God does ever be boring?

To be fair, some teachers succeed in making it appear dull, which is tragic, as well as irresponsible. But a believer's grasp of theological truths is a matter of urgent prayer.

Paul's first focus is on God's plan for us.

"We continually ask God to fill you with the knowledge of his will through all the wisdom and understanding that the Spirit gives." (**v 9**)

This is not a one-off prayer but something he is committed to praying "continually". Remember, these are young believers who have started well in their faith. God has granted them new birth as the result of Epaphras' gospel preaching. But that is no ground for complacency. Ministry can never be simply about converts completing response cards at an event—it is about making and supporting lifelong disciples. The need to be filled with the knowledge of God's will is constant. But what does that mean exactly? Is this primarily a matter of guidance, so that we discover what God wants from us on a day to day basis? That is certainly how this verse is sometimes taken. Of course, it is vital, and right, to lean on God for his direction in big life decisions—like those about work, marriage, future service and so on. Yet Paul's weighty prayer here points to something different but even greater.

Paul tends to write about the will of God for believers in universal rather than individualistic terms. In stark contrast to worldly thinking and living (see Romans 12:1-2 or Ephesians 5:15-17), "It is God's will that you should be sanctified" (1 Thessalonians 4:3) and, "Rejoice always, pray continually, give thanks in all circumstances; for this is God's will for you in Christ Jesus" (1 Thessalonians 5:16-18). To be sanctified is to live consistently with one's identity as a "saint", that is a person who belongs to God, as we saw in the previous section.

It is perhaps now easier to understand why this prayer must be continual. There is always room for improvement when it comes to being like our heavenly Father. So, we could say that to know God's will is effectively to know God's character. The two always go together in the Bible, as the Ten Commandments illustrate (see Exodus 20:1-17). For example, the command not to commit adultery reflects God's

> To know God's will is effectively to know God's character. The two always go together in the Bible.

own faithfulness to his promises; the command not to envy others reflects God's commitment to generous provision. But even the first four commandments (which relate to our relationship to our Creator)

> To understand what God wants we need to know what God is like. To know what God is like we need to spend time with him.

illustrate God's nature. After all, if he is the only true God, it is entirely consistent to say we should never worship others.

To understand what God wants we need to know what God is like. To know what God is like we need to spend time with him, listening to what he says. This marks the difference between theology as a dry, cerebral pursuit (the sole object of which is clever and complicated statements) and theology as a living, breathing way of life. It is all about our relationship with God. No wonder this is an important prayer. It is one prayer that God longs to answer.

The key word here is "wisdom".

Our contemporary world seems to have forgotten wisdom's value. If people talk about it at all, they usually confuse it with knowledge.

■ We drown in a sea of data: demographic statistics, quarterly sales results, hours of battery life. You name it, there is data about it. But raw data by itself gets us nowhere if we don't know what to do with it.

■ Once we see connections between different parts of the data, we have information. This describes the nature of reality out there. But information alone is not that helpful. We need to know its significance.

■ So we pool together what information we can to form what can then be called knowledge. Knowledge is about grasping

WISDOM

KNOWLEDGE

INFORMATION

DATA

the meaning of that reality, the significance of the information at our disposal.

- So far so good—but none of that tells us what to do now. For that we need wisdom. Wisdom is about knowing what action or behaviour is good, what is beneficial, what is healthy. It cannot be learned from a book or reduced to a theoretical soundbite. It takes years of experience and insight, years of success and especially of failure. That is why the wisest in society are usually reckoned to be those who have lived longest.

So you can mine the internet for all kinds of data, and are even able to rattle off streams of memorised facts and figures. You can know the average length of battery life for your type of phone, for example. You might even remember how long the charge lasted a week ago. But that by itself is pointless if you don't know what to do with it. In other words, the wise thing is to plug it into a power source every now and then.

Memorising swathes of theology serves little purpose if it stays as head knowledge. The grandest purpose of theological knowledge must be to pursue godly wisdom. What is the best way to gain wisdom? Surely, it is to spend time with wise people! And there is no one wiser than our God. So Paul's continual prayer in Colossians **1:9** is for God, by his Spirit, to give us both knowledge and the wisdom and understanding to know what to do with it.

Paul does not pray for the Colossians to have a quick fix, but for God to do a lifelong work. Paul is in the discipleship business. What does he hope will result?

"… so that you may live a life worthy of the Lord and please him in every way: bearing fruit in every good work, growing in the knowledge of God." (**v 10**)

A life worthy of the God who has called us to be his. Notice how unrestricted he is here. It is the whole of life that is to be worthy; it is to please God in every way—to produce every good work. This includes the big set-piece events that everyone sees—like preaching at a guest service or organising the church's care for homeless people; and also the invisible and small ones—the quiet text to a friend who is struggling or the way we bring up our children. It includes the way we drive our cars as well as how we treat those with irritating jobs like telephone marketers or airport officials. There is no part of life that is excluded from the call to please God.

There is a kind of **virtuous circle** at work here. Paul prays for the knowledge of God's will that brings godly wisdom—which itself leads to a worthy and pleasing life. But then, the more we live like that, the more we will actually get to know God better! We prove him right and so we trust him more.

## 2. With God's power for patient perseverance

After reflecting on his victory at Waterloo in 1815, the Duke of Wellington remarked magnanimously, "Our men were not braver than the enemy. They were merely brave five minutes longer." He was a realist. True warriors know how tough battles get.

Paul wants every Christian to endure to the end. It means keeping going in faith, love and hope until the thing we hope for has been attained. Notice that these paragraphs (**v 3-13**) constantly have that end point in view. But that is an intimidating thought—especially if the battle with temptation or opposition rages fiercely. How do we keep on bearing the fruit of good works then? Look how he continues:

"… being strengthened with all power according to his glorious might so that you may have great endurance and patience." (**v 11**)

We are never abandoned to fight this battle alone. Just as the Spirit fills us with wisdom and understanding, so he enables the very perseverance he calls us to. In fact, the most powerful evidence for his invisible work must surely be the fact that believers still believe despite their horrendous circumstances. Like the Romanian Richard Wurmbrand, who endured 11 years of solitary confinement in a communist prison; or my East African friend with an aristocratic Muslim background, who lives under threat of death from his family for his bold proclamation of the Christian faith; or the teenager who endures the malicious jeers of school friends for her faith but keeps coming to the church youth group.

It doesn't matter what the battle is—if we are in the middle of it, it is still tough. We feel alone. The future seems bleak. The pressure looks set only to increase. But this is precisely the moment to turn to the Lord (even if that is the last thing we feel like doing). It is all the more important to pray these things for others.

So perhaps, as Paul did for the Colossians, you could learn about a minority Christian community in another part of the world and commit to pray for their growth in wisdom and perseverance. It makes no difference that you are never likely to meet them. That never stopped Paul from rolling up his sleeves in prayer for churches. There are many agencies and organisations that offer this kind of information, so ignorance of what is going on out there is really no excuse.

Paul knew that the Colossians had made the first steps of faith and so he prayed for them to carry on through to the end. He didn't seek converts but disciples, and their perseverance was the surest sign of the Spirit's work.

## 3. In joyful gratitude for kingdom glory

If this prayer has so far made the Christian life seem like drudgery, then the next verses put us straight. Perseverance might be hard, but it pales in comparison with what we already have in Christ and what we can look forward to in Christ. This is why Paul bursts with gratitude to the Father for the news from Colossae (**v 12**).

Then suddenly, Paul's gratitude for the Colossian believers seems to

There has been a revolution in their lives, bringing a transformation as total as the difference between night and day.

launch his imagination into the stratosphere. This is because he does not regard them only as citizens of a far-flung provincial Roman town. Nor does he think they have made a supposedly peculiar lifestyle choice about what god or gods to believe or reject. Still less does he think they have been deluded or conned. He is convinced that an event with cosmic reverberations has taken place. There has been a revolution in their lives, bringing a transformation as total as the difference between night and day. Why? Because God "has qualified you to share in the inheritance of his holy people in the kingdom of light" (**v 12**).

Qualifications are a modern obsession. It is perfectly understandable when the jobs market is so competitive, of course, especially in a globalised world. In a dog-eat-dog culture, the only way to get ahead is to prove that I am superior to all rivals. So, an obvious route to self-promotion (apart from the traditional methods of birth into a well-connected family or collecting contacts) is to accumulate letters after your name. I know one friend who, after her law degree, qualified as a lawyer; she then decided to train as an accountant, passing with flying colours; and now, as if that wasn't enough, she is doing a theology degree in her spare time. Useful for defending a Christian who ends up in court for **tithing** on their tax return perhaps! What is clear, though, is that each set of letters after her name represents months and months of long and lonely study. She is truly qualified!

So what qualifications can Paul have in mind for sharing in God's "kingdom of light"? He says that this inheritance comes to "holy people". Does that mean we need to obtain a certain level of holiness? And if so, how holy must we be? Is it a bit like the Olympic high jump, where we need to get into training and reach a basic minimum to get into the games? Or is it more a matter of studying for theology exams?

That is certainly what many imagine Christianity to be: a religion for good people, and for which the "bad" need not apply. "I'm not good enough for church," someone may think or say when we invite them to join us on Sunday.

There are so many things wrong with this view that it is hard to know where to begin. First, it never originated with Jesus himself. He spent most of his time with the "sinners and tax collectors" (as they were labelled in his day) whereas it was the religious, "churchy" types who orchestrated his execution. The second problem is how to measure goodness. How good is good enough? Most of us pitch ourselves somewhere roughly between Stalin and Mother Theresa, and hope for the best. But, supposing the holiness pass mark is 50%, what happens if I only get 49% holy? That's still quite a lot of holiness—just not quite enough. And anyway, since when was anything less than perfection appropriate for God?

The remarkable, even miraculous, truth of the Christian gospel is that this kind of discussion is entirely unnecessary and futile. Look again at **verse 12** and notice why gratitude can be the only appropriate response. This qualification is granted—never earned. The Father does the qualifying. He gives us the status of holy people (ESV: "saints") in the first place. Which is just as well, because since we are all trapped within the dominion of darkness, we ourselves have no means of escape to the kingdom of light. It is impossible.

As he says in **verses 13-14**, "he has rescued us from the dominion of darkness and brought us into the kingdom of the Son he loves, in whom we have redemption, the forgiveness of sins". He has not only made the impossible possible; he has made it available even to us today. How else could we, who cannot make ourselves holy, get qualified? Even if I decide to turn over a new leaf today, I still have my years of sin and rebellion behind me to deal with, and no one can change the past. But God in Christ offers forgiveness for all that—

> God in Christ offers forgiveness— which means that nobody ever has to be a slave of their history.

which means that nobody ever has to be a slave of their history.

This marks nothing less than a transfer of cosmic citizenship. In the spiritual realms of the universe, there are no human empires—there is one ultimate battle between darkness and light. But the ruler of the dominion of darkness is much more subtle than human powers because he prefers to skulk around in the shadows, without its subjects even being aware of his existence. But the dark dominion certainly makes its presence felt as soon as God's kingdom surfaces. The last thing it wants is for people to flee to and seek asylum in the light. The only hope is for rescue to be achieved and won on our behalf. That is precisely what the Lord Jesus has done. His victory has repercussions that thread through the whole of what Paul writes in Colossians and Philemon.

We must read on to learn more about how he has done this and what it means for us. But for now, Paul is clear. This calls for overwhelmed gratitude to God. What Christ did for us in his first coming, ultimately at the cross and resurrection, gives us full confidence that we will be loved, accepted and welcomed when he returns at his second coming.

# Questions for reflection

1. Think of someone you consider to be truly wise. What is it about them, their understanding and way of thinking that you value? How could you grow more like them?

2. When was the last time you thanked God for the faith, love and hope of your friends and family? Or prayed for these things to grow?

3. "It's one thing to be grateful. It's another to give thanks. Gratitude is what you feel. Thanksgiving is what you do" (Tim Keller). How can you grow a sense of genuine gratitude in your heart? How can improve the way you express your gratitude in thanksgiving?

# 2. CHRIST THE UNIVERSAL

I could never be Jewish, even if I was born a Jew or had Jewish ancestry.

That may seem a strange, if not offensive, thing to say. Yet according to some modern definitions, it is a fact. The simple reason is that I have become convinced that Jesus is Immanuel (Hebrew for "God among us"). Yes—I believe that he was, and is, divine. And therein lies the problem.

Since the creation of the modern nation state of Israel in 1948, a founding principle has been the right of Jewish people to live in the territory. The "Law of Return" was enacted just two years later, primarily to ensure a Jewish majority. Anyone with at least one Jewish grandparent was permitted to gain citizenship. It was a successful policy, and millions took up the offer.

Inevitably, debates arose about how to define Jewishness, coming to a head in a crisis in the 1950s that rocked the Israeli government. The Israeli Supreme Court eventually defined a Jew as someone born Jewish "as long as he or she does not accept another religion". Fair enough perhaps, but the agenda was not hard to discern. Under these rules, applicants can be atheist and qualify as Jewish, but once they accept Jesus as **Messiah**, they forfeit that eligibility, even if they believe in the existence of God and the authority of the Old Testament. It is ironic. As one writer said:

"It is the rejection of Jesus as Christ that binds American Jews together. It is by the rejection of the messiahship of

Jesus that we proclaim to the world that we are still Jews."

(Stan Telchin, *Abandoned,* page 100)

It is extraordinary. I have friends who see themselves as Messianic Jews, precisely because they see Jesus as the fulfilment of everything they ever were and longed for as Jewish people. But the state of Israel rejects them. Legally, they are no longer Jews.

But I cannot stop there. I could never be a **Unitarian**, a **Mormon**, a **Muslim** or a **Hindu** either. All for the same reason: because I am convinced that Jesus is the one true God. Some would say I am mad or worse; others that I've committed intellectual suicide. Many imagine they could never believe what I believe. For as Mahatma Gandhi once said:

"I cannot ascribe exclusive divinity to Jesus. He is as divine as Krishna or Rama or Mohammed or Zoroaster."

In other words, he is no more, nor less, divine than anyone else. People are quick to remind us that convictions like mine lead to wars, bloodshed and disharmony in society. And who can deny it? Exclusive claims do often lead to conflict.

However, awkward though it is to point this out, Gandhi's statement simply doesn't fit the plain facts about Jesus and his claims. The great science-fiction novelist H.G. Wells wrote, "I am an historian, I am not a believer, but … this penniless preacher from Nazareth is irrevocably the very centre of history." Or take T.S. Eliot, who did become a believer in later life. He alluded to Jesus in his *Burnt Norton* (from *The Four Quartets*) as "the still point of a turning world".

Those are not **relative** statements. They are **categorical**, emphatic, and, dare I say it, **universal**. And that is scandalous.

> Colossians is a scandalous text, and perhaps more unpalatable today than ever.

Colossians is a scandalous text, and perhaps more unpalatable today than ever. It unrelentingly collides with modern assumptions. To state what Paul asserts today sounds as pea-brained and offensive as claiming racial superiority for Northern Europeans or that the sun orbits the earth. The first is appalling racism, the second half-witted ignorance. We are constantly told that no religion today has the right, let alone the ability, to make any exclusive claims whatsoever. So, to modern ears, Colossians sounds offensive or ludicrous. And this offence is nowhere more startling than Colossians 1:15-20.

## Paul's "universals"

To grasp just how shocking Paul's claims are, conducting a simple observation exercise of his opening paragraphs is a good way to start. Spot the use of "universals" in chapter 1: all, every, whole and full. Quite an impressive list emerges.

- **v 6:** "… the gospel is bearing fruit and growing throughout the *whole* world…"

- **v 9:** "We continually ask God to fill you with the knowledge of his will through *all* the wisdom and understanding…"

- **v 10:** "… so that you may … please him in *every* way: bearing fruit in *every* good work."

- **v 11:** "… being strengthened with *all* power."

We might be tempted to think that **verse 6** is an example of the tendency to exaggeration that is common to many **evangelists** the world over. After all, around AD 60, the church had spread to only a relatively small proportion of the globe. But we would be wrong. There is an indication from Luke's construction of the book of Acts around Acts 1:8 that once the gospel reached Rome (as symbolised by Paul's preaching there in Acts 28), this represented reaching "the ends of the earth". The cumulative effect of the other universals that follow in the paragraph that this chapter focuses on cannot be put down to mere exaggeration.

- Colossians **1:15:** "The Son is … the firstborn over *all* creation."

- **v 16:** "For in him *all* things were created … *all* things have been created through him and for him."

- **v 17:** "He is before *all* things, and in him *all* things hold together."

- **v 18:** "… so that in *everything* he might have the supremacy."

- **v 19:** "For God was pleased to have *all* his fullness dwell in him."

- **v 20:** "… and through him to reconcile to himself *all* things."

It's hard to miss his point now. Paul claims a message of absolute relevance to every person in every nation in every era. This obviously includes the Colossian Christians—together with their **pagan** neighbours. This also includes you as you read this—together with your family, neighbours, colleagues, and even your casual acquaintances and those you just walk past on the street.

Just let that sink in for a moment.

Bring to mind all the people you encounter in the course of an average week. Especially those you barely give a moment's thought to: the bus or train driver working unsocial hours; the homeless man who's always sitting outside the same coffee shop; the parents at the school gate so preoccupied with caring for their child with Down's syndrome that they have no energy to befriend other parents; the local politician you run into while she campaigns in the street. The list goes on. And so does Jesus' authority.

Abraham Kuyper was an extraordinary man. Before his death at 83 in 1920, he had been a pastor who founded a church denomination, a journalist who started a national newspaper, a theologian and writer who started a university, and a politician who founded his own political party and who became Prime Minister of the Netherlands for four years! That is quite a legacy. What could have motivated such an obviously capable and driven man? No doubt there were many aspects of it, but above all it was surely his convictions about Jesus Christ. He is perhaps most famous today for this crucial insight, which he shared during his inaugural lecture at the Free University of Amsterdam:

"no single piece of our mental world is to be hermetically sealed off from the rest, and there is not a square inch in the whole domain of our human existence over which Christ, who is **Sovereign** over all, does not cry: 'Mine!'"

Jesus is concerned for every aspect of every life of every creature. He is truly the Lord.

What exactly does that mean? Paul picks up two key elements, which we will now explore in this and the next part of this chapter. The first is Jesus' relationship to creation.

## Jesus the Creator: firstborn over all creation

Ancient Jews would never have struggled to believe that there is only one God and that he created everything that exists. For starters, Genesis chapters 1 – 2 make that perfectly clear. But for the many in Colossae from a pagan background, the idea would have been palpably absurd. They followed many gods and had many myths about the world's origins.

But the idea that this unique Creator actually spent time on earth would have baffled both groups. Yet that is precisely what Paul insists had happened just a few years before.

### 1. Know Jesus of Nazareth, know God the Father

God is invisible. But **paradoxically**, the Son is "the image of the invisible God" (Colossians **1:15**), meaning that he makes the invisible visible. If you wanted to know what I am like, you could start by typing my name into Google and looking at my photograph—at my image. So it is with God. If you want to know what God is like, you need to look at his Son—because he is God's true image. Or in the words of Hebrews, he is "the exact representation of his being" (Hebrews 1:3). Like a great portrait, Jesus offers a true likeness of the Father.

It is a bit like visiting a great medieval cathedral famous for its magnificent vaulted ceiling. It is covered in intricate stonework as well as the emblems of important benefactors and stonemasons. Stare at it too long and you will get a cricked neck. Consequently, scores of visitors leave without the slightest sense of the glories above. Tourist-savvy institutions therefore provide slanted mirrors on trolleys, so that visitors can move around for as long as they want and look down in order to see what is up above. Jesus is like one of those slanted mirrors—we look at him and can see what is far beyond our range of sight.

But of course, this illustration only works up to a point. He is far more than a mere picture of God. He actually is God. He is not simply God's representative on earth (as the ambassador of a foreign country is a representative of his home state). He is God on earth. So the next time someone asks you if you have ever seen God, the answer is simple. "No, of course not. But I would have done if I'd lived in Judea 2000 years ago!"

Some are troubled by Paul's next words, since they appear to contradict what he has just said. Jesus is "the firstborn over all creation" (Colossians **1:15**). Some, including **Jehovah's Witnesses** (following the ancient **heresy** of **Arianism**) take this to mean that Jesus of Nazareth was a creature like you and me—a human being but no more. He is special, we are told, because of his unique authority as "firstborn over all creation". But he is merely first among equals. He is certainly not divine.

There are at least two reasons why this cannot be Paul's point: the significance of the word "firstborn", and the subsequent verses.

"Firstborn" had a specific connotation in Paul's day. It described the rights associated with being the main inheritor of a family's wealth. In the majority of cases, that person was the firstborn son, but there could be exceptions. The main point of this word picture is the fact that this individual inherits, rather than who his biological father is. So Paul is saying that Jesus of Nazareth is the inheritor of all creation by right.

Why is that?

## 2. Know Jesus of Nazareth, know the Creator of everything

The simple answer is that he made it all. "For in him all things were created," Paul writes (**v 16**). It is a staggering claim. Yet it stands to reason. If a great artist paints a masterpiece, he or she has full owner-ship rights over it, right up until the moment it is sold to a collector or given to a friend. Well, Jesus has never done that with his master-piece. He never would. He made everything. So he owns everything.

And by "everything", Paul really does mean everything:

"things in heaven and on earth, visible and invisible, whether thrones or powers or rulers or authorities; all things have been created through him and for him." (**v 16**)

This therefore includes the microscopic and cosmic; the physical and spiritual; the biological and geological; even the human and demonic. The entire Roman Empire, from the North Sea to the Black Sea, was under his **sway** as its Creator. The satanic realm of deception and evil is under his sway as its Creator. The entire cosmos of stars and constellations is under his sway as its Creator.

Of course, that provokes the question of how on earth that could be consistent with his integrity and goodness, but that will have to wait until later in Colossians.

For now, one thing is abundantly clear. Kuyper was spot on: it is all his because he made it all.

I hope there are aspects of our world that still astound you. Perhaps it is breathtaking scenes in nature documentaries such as the vast animal stampedes across Africa's savannahs; or the wonder of birds that can migrate thousands of miles to precisely the same nesting spot; or the intricate but always unique beauty of a snowflake. Or perhaps it is simply the freshness of a sunny spring morning. It doesn't matter what it is. What matters is that all that is beautiful and inspiring about the world is that way because Jesus made it like that.

## 3. Know Jesus of Nazareth, know the Sustainer of everything

As if that wasn't enough to boggle the mind, then Paul's next point surely will stretch it to breaking point. Jesus, this astonishing man, who walked throughout ancient Judea, who got his feet muddy in the River Jordan, and who enjoyed a wedding feast with friends and family, existed before it all began (**v 17**).

This explains that pin-drop moment when Jesus yet again found himself in a tangle with religious leaders. Abraham was, of course, Israel's founding father. Every Jewish person could trace descent from him. So, when questions arose about the origins of Jesus' authority, it is not hard to see how inflammatory his responses were. He claimed to know Abraham personally, and that Abraham "rejoiced at the thought of seeing my day…" (John 8:56). To top it all…

> "'Very truly I tell you,' Jesus answered, 'before Abraham was born, I am!' At this, they picked up stones to stone him, but Jesus hid himself, slipping away from the temple grounds."
>
> (John 8:58-59)

This wasn't simply arrogance, still less a poor grasp of grammatical tenses. It was **blasphemy**. But only if it was a falsehood. Jesus was asserting his existence before creation, and thus his divinity. Even the way he phrased it—"I am"—alludes to God's revealed name, Yahweh (meaning "I am who I am"). That is why these leaders felt entirely justified in preparing to stone him. Jesus was outrageous.

Last but not least, according to Paul, Jesus keeps the universe going. Gravity may well exert the most extraordinary forces on everything from insects to planets, yet Jesus Christ, fully God and fully man, is the one on whom it depends second by second. As Paul says, "In him all things hold together" (Colossians **1:17**) This is not simply an idea to explain the aspects of our universe that science cannot explain. God works through those that we can explain too! Instead, the Bible writers' conviction was that God's creative power is not only seen in some ancient one-off event but is ongoing. God is actively involved in sustaining his creation moment by moment. Without him, everything would revert to the nothingness and chaos that existed before God got to work in Genesis 1. Jesus is at work all around us at every single moment.

It seems absurd and impossible to grasp. Yet that is no less than what Paul claims for the one he worships.

After this condensed catalogue of Jesus' qualifications, it is no wonder that he has all the rights due to the "firstborn over all creation".

## Questions for reflection

1. Why would people find the statements in this passage so outrageous? What might you say in response to someone who thought these claims ridiculous?

2. Jesus is the image of the invisible God: how would you explain to someone what Christians believe about Jesus and his deity?

3. Jesus is the sustainer: how should this knowledge change the way we view both Jesus and the universe we live in?

## PART TWO

# Christ the universal:
# irreconcilable, reconciled

It should now be obvious why Jesus stamps everything with the word "Mine!" He made it all. Yet this truth only serves to ratchet up a problem: if it is all his, why doesn't he do something about everything that has gone so badly wrong?

As I write this, various events have taken place to mark the centenary of the Russian Revolution. It was a time of terrifying turbulence: a deadly cocktail of outlandish optimism and ruthless politics. While the world was caught up in the horrors of the First World War, Lenin and his comrades seized their opportunity with both hands. It was easy to attract support, at least at the start, because the tsars had oppressed the people for centuries in a cruelly rigid class structure. The majority of Russians lived in what was slavery in all but name. Something just had to change. And violence seemed the only way to make it happen because the ruling class, from Tsar Nicholas II down, resisted even the tiniest of reforms at every turn. Yet no sooner had the Russian people been liberated from one dictatorial regime, than they discovered that they were oppressed by another. Millions suffered and died. And yet, Jesus Christ is Lord of all…

A quarter of a century later, the world was engulfed in *another* world war. The second would prove even worse than the first. But here is the real tragedy that too often gets forgotten: whatever happened, a **totalitarian** regime would be on the winning side. It was impossible for both Hitler and Stalin to lose.

- Hitler was responsible for six million Jewish deaths, as well as countless others through military aggression and Nazi occupation.

- Stalin was directly responsible for around seven million deaths (or perhaps as many as twelve million) during the notorious 1933 Ukrainian famine (the direct result of the savage manipulation of food distribution). Then there were the countless millions who disappeared into the Gulag; the vast system of Siberian prison camps.

How do you choose between the two? This is not to say that the Western allies could always claim the moral high ground—for no global power has ever kept its hands clean from corruption, injustice and cruelty. Yet nothing in the West quite reached the sheer scale of this horror. And yet, Jesus Christ is Lord of all…

Looking back over the past century, then, it is hard to hold back the tears and rage. And that is before we have even started on the likes of Ceauşescu, Mao, Pol Pot, Idi Amin, Mobutu, Pinochet, Saddam Hussein, Muammar Gaddafi. And yet, Jesus Christ is Lord of all…

What do we do with this?

Of course, Paul had no illusions about the Roman Empire: a regime that could be just as ruthless and cruel as more modern examples. He was its prisoner! There were benefits to citizenship, to be sure, and he made full use of them to serve God's kingdom. But even in his day, the regime showed little love for Christ and no respect for Christ's authority. This never stopped Paul from asserting that Jesus Christ is Lord of all. He had few doubts about that, in large part because of what he goes on to write. Human powers may well continue to commit atrocities and injustices, but Christ is all too aware of what is going on.

## Jesus the rescuer: firstborn over the new creation

We now get to the heart of why the cosmic Creator would ever desire to become a creature. It is an act that gives us a glimpse into God's breathtaking genius. For by becoming human, Jesus simultaneously showed both how seriously he takes the devastation we have wrought in his world and how much he values us, his creatures. But the evidence for both of these vitally important truths comes from a very surprising place: *the church.*

Ask the person in the street what they make of "the church" today, and their answers will be many and varied. But few, if any, would come even close to suggesting that it is proof of divine genius. The more positive might dwell on the church's psychological and social benefits for its members, and even its positive impact on surrounding communities. On the other hand, pointing to declining numbers and media scandals, some might focus on the dangers of organised religion. It's no different from any other flawed human institution, and so deserves to wither into irrelevance, they might say.

If you were asked about your own church, it is unlikely that you would leave God's purpose out of the picture as completely as these contemporary perspectives do. But would you see it as evidence of God's genius? See what Paul has to say.

## A parallel authority

Just as Jesus made the cosmos, so Jesus made the church. The words and structure of Colossians **1:18-20** deliberately echo those of verses 15-17. The implication, therefore, is that the church is the starting point for God's new creation. Its very existence assures us that everything will be remade, restored, renewed.

- Jesus' authority over creation is echoed by his authority over the new creation: "he is the head of the body, the church" (**v 18**).

- Jesus' right to inherit his creation is echoed by his rights over the new creation: "He is the beginning and the firstborn from among the dead".

- The totality of Jesus' rule over creation is echoed by his rule over the new creation: "… that in everything he might have the supremacy".

But this still does not actually explain why it was necessary for Jesus to become human. The first clue lies in the phrase "firstborn from among the dead". Bizarre though it sounds, Jesus "inherits" all those who have survived death, precisely because he is the first person to have conquered death. He proves that there is life beyond this life. But the fact that death exists at all reveals the reality of something having gone very badly wrong in God's creation. That was never God's design. The world today is not how God first created it to be.

## A divine presence

Paul then picks up on his previous statement in **verse 15** about Jesus' nature as God's image. He now explains how it was possible for him to reveal God's true nature. "For God was pleased to have all his fullness dwell in him," he writes (**v 19**). It's a strange way of putting it perhaps—the idea is that God has taken up permanent residence in Jesus. But there are no half-measures here. It is yet another of Paul's "universals". This time, his subject is not the scope of Jesus' authority but the basis of his identity. Of course, these words should never be dislocated from their context to suggest that there was ever a point at which God's fullness did not dwell in the Son. That would be absurd in the context of everything else Paul teaches here. His point is surely that God was simply delighted for his fullness to be expressed in his Son as a human being. He had no reservations about that whatsoever.

> The fact that death exists at all reveals the reality of something having gone very badly wrong in God's creation.

This is breathtaking. It is impossible to find the words that capture it adequately. But I love these concise words of the seventeenth-century preacher-poet John Donne that somehow nail it:

> 'Twas much, that man was made like God before,
> But that God should be like man much more.

This was a crucial point for the Colossian believers to grasp. The ancient Greek mindset took a highly negative view of all things physical and bodily. It is not hard to see why. After all, in a culture that most prized the more "spiritual" realm of ideas and the mind, the body seems to let the side down. Bodies have an irritating tendency to embarrass us with their uncontrollable smells, sounds and emissions; that is before we even consider our flaws and limits, especially as we get older and weaker. Then our bodies grind to an ignominious halt altogether when we breathe our last. It's hardly a glorious story. Surely it is better to think deep, profound and beautiful thoughts, and encourage everyone to do the same.

But no. That is not God's style. He created the body and so is quite prepared—no, more than that, he is entirely pleased—to embrace the reality of having a body. Bodies cannot be so bad after all, it seems. God's purpose in becoming fully human goes far beyond simply proving that, however. He was pleased for this precisely because he was pleased to rescue his creation. And becoming human was fundamental to achieving that—even if it meant dying like the rest of us; or, to be more accurate, precisely because he would die like the rest of us.

## A victorious sacrifice

Bleeding was a serious matter in the ancient world. Even the slightest cut could be lethal because of the possibility of infection. We take our antibiotics, antiseptics and sterile operations entirely for granted, confident that most ailments can be fixed with a pill or a swab. But that simply wasn't the case even just a few generations back. The sight of blood was a serious matter. This is why Leviticus insisted that "the life of every creature is its blood" (Leviticus 17:14), because when blood oozes out of a wound rather than pumping around the body, death is not far off.

But in Old Testament times, the sight of blood often represented something worse: a violent death. Jesus' death was supremely violent. It came in response to the sentence of a **kangaroo court**, after extreme verbal and physical abuse, and involved the most barbaric form of torturous execution. Paul alludes to all of that in his phrase "his blood, shed on the cross" (Colossians **1:20**). It comes as a shock, then, to discover that not only was this central to God's plan in the

Son becoming human, but also that this brutal end might actually achieve something.

For blood had an even greater significance. In the temple system, the blood from a sacrificial offering symbolised God's gift of a sub-stitute: one death in the place of another to provide freedom from judgment. When an animal's blood was smeared on Israelite door-frames in Egypt, this was a sign to God that there had been a death in that household (see Exodus 12:21-23). The family had taken God's warning of his imminent judgment seriously. They had taken him at his word and so they performed the sacrifice and painted the blood (despite that being a very peculiar thing to do in itself).

> "On that same night I will pass through Egypt and strike down every firstborn of both people and animals, and I will bring judg-ment on all the gods of Egypt. I am the LORD. The blood will be a sign for you on the houses where you are, and when I see the blood, I will pass over you. No destructive plague will touch you when I strike Egypt." (Exodus 12:12-13)

One death in place of another: God's template for dealing with the threat we face from his justice.

The modern world rates peacemakers very highly, and rightly so. To bring about change while resisting violence is no small achievement. People are quick to hail the likes of Gandhi, Martin Luther King and Nel-son Mandela, but one figure who has too quickly been forgotten is the late King Hus-sein of Jordan. He was a key player in the Middle East peace process, involved behind the scenes in the run-up to the 1978 Camp David Accords between Israel and Egypt. Here was a monarch who was determined to do all he could to bring about the recon-ciliation of sworn enemies.

Yet nobody would ever have suggested to him that his best contribution to the

**One death in place of another: God's template for dealing with the threat we face from his justice.**

peace process might be his death. What an insult! He could only actually help by living. To suggest otherwise would be absurd. And yet, a sacrificial death was precisely the means by which God's King would bring about cosmic reconciliation. How come?

Ever since Genesis 3, the root cause of all that is wrong in the world—from the grand scale of empires and nations right down to the personal level of playground bullies and marital conflict—is simple. It is sin. This is the human heart-attitude that consistently chooses to go it alone. It is a matter of creatures declaring independence from the Creator. We insist that we don't need God or his ways in our lives. Everything needs to be done our own way. That is treason of a cosmic order.

The problem then is that everyone plays the same game, and the results are horrendous. Just read a newspaper. If everyone is asserting their independence and supremacy over everyone else, people will get hurt. If there is to be any peace, there must be at least an admission of who has done what.

One thing we can be clear on, however. Jesus Christ, Creator and Sustainer of all that exists, is not to blame. He has nothing to repent of, nothing to confess. It is we who have rejected him. That cosmic sin needs to be named and shamed—he cannot simply overlook it as if it were irrelevant. The havoc we have wreaked in the world is bad enough. But the personal affront to the One on whom we depend for our very breath is the worst of it. Justice demands a facing up to truth and the imposition of the right penalty. If we reject our Creator, we deserve our Creator's rejection.

It seems like a dead end. There is nothing we can do about our problem.

But this is where the miracle of the gospel begins to gleam in all its glory. Jesus takes the initiative, to do for us what we could never do for ourselves.

## Summary: Jesus is unique

- *Jesus is uniquely qualified to reconcile us:* Because Jesus is fully God, he therefore has the power to take the initiative to bring us back to himself. He alone has the authority to show mercy to rebels against him and forgive. Even more significantly, because he is fully human, he knows what it is really like to be us. He has come down to our level and can relate to every aspect of life on earth. That is crucial, because in any reconciliation negotiations, it is vital for those involved to understand the perspectives of all sides. The one who is fully God and fully man is able then to bring both sides together.

- *Jesus uniquely sacrificed himself to reconcile us to God.* Because Jesus shed his blood on the cross, nothing remains to add. He has died the death that my sin deserved. To take the words of Paul in Colossians **1:12**, it is Christ's cross that has "qualified us" for the kingdom of light. This is what brought our "redemption, the forgiveness of sins" (**v 14**). This explains Christ's great victory cry in death: "It is finished" (John 19:30). At last, it becomes possible for rebel creatures to return to where we belong—in dependent relationship with our Creator.

Note that this heads off those who would attack this **doctrine** by suggesting that Jesus is some sort of **innocent third party**, dragged kicking and screaming by a vengeful God to take our punishment which he did not deserve. As Paul wrote to the Corinthian believers, because Jesus is fully God, he was intimately involved with both creating the plan and executing it. "God was reconciling the world to himself in Christ, not counting people's sins against them" (2 Corinthians 5:19).

If we have any doubts that the cross really was enough, Paul dispels them immediately. Calvary has truly cosmic scope. The cross is the means by which God can "reconcile to himself all things, whether things on earth or things in heaven" (Colossians **1:20**). This is universal reconciliation—a new creation which overturns all that has gone wrong in the first creation. Would that the world would recognise it!

The extraordinary thing is that the evidence of God's work of new creation is the existence of the church. This does not simply mean the Church with a capital "C" that is, the body of believers drawn from every nation and generation. God's evidence includes the church that meets down the street where you live; and the local congregation that you are perhaps part of; and the fellowship nearby that gets up to some slightly whacky activities that you don't fully understand or accept; plus the tiny group of brothers and sisters forced to meet in secret because of an oppressive government regime; not to mention the church that seems staid and formal, and is opposed to any music written after 1700. All of these are expressions of God's people living out their faith. As such, all are evidence that God is bringing about a new creation.

What God is doing in the church is the focus of the rest of what Paul wants to say in this letter. But for now, we can summarise the wonders of these verses like this. There is a clear parallel between the first creation and the new creation. In both we see Christ at work and reigning supreme. He is the one for whom both "creations" exist—which is why he inherits both as the firstborn. Without Christ, there would be no cosmos and no church. Neither would have been created, neither would be sustainable. He is the universal Lord of all.

|  | First Creation (1:15-17) | New Creation (1:18-20) |
| --- | --- | --- |
| **Christ's Nature** | Image of the invisible God (1:15) | God was pleased ... His fullness dwells in Him (1:19) |
| **Christ's Inheritance** | Firstborn over all creation (1:15) | Firstborn from among the dead (1:18) |
| **Christ's Authority** | Over all creation (1:15) | In everything ... the supremacy (1:18) |
| **Christ's Indispensability** | In him all things hold together (1:17) | Head of the body, the church (1:18) |
| **Christ's Universality** | All things have been created through him and for him (1:16) | Reconcile all things ... through His blood (1:20) |

## Questions for reflection

1. How do you feel about the significance of church in general, and your church in particular? How have the ideas of this chapter changed those views?

2. Could you explain in a way that a non-believer could understand the reasons why Jesus had to become a living, breathing human being in order to save us?

3. How does Jesus' death on the cross make peace? What do people still find offensive about that claim?

# 3. THE COSMIC, RECONCILED

It's not only teenagers who experience FOMO (Fear Of Missing Out). It can happen to any of us. It is that brutal sense you get when you discover that everyone in the office has been invited to a get-together—except you. Or that rising panic after hanging around for hours waiting for information on plane or train delays—only to realise that everyone else you had spotted who was waiting with you has suddenly disappeared. "What do they know that I don't? Am I going to miss my connection now? Will I be stuck here for weeks?"

These are intensely unpleasant experiences. Yet, while grim, their effects are unlikely to be long-lasting.

But what about missing out on something that *is* long-lasting? And what if there was nothing you could do about it? How would you cope then?

That is precisely the situation that Paul describes in our next section.

## Excluded—permanently?

The great Jerusalem Temple dominated the ancient city, especially after King Herod's mammoth renovations begun around two decades before the birth of Christ. Whatever street you were on, it loomed large: a vast architectural wonder with profound theological significance, making permanent the old **tabernacle** (or tent) from of old.

Its basic message was clear: *Yahweh, the God who revealed his name to Israel through Moses, is here, dwelling at the heart of his people.* In the capital city, you couldn't miss the point. No wonder the **psalmist** sees Zion, the mountain on which the temple stood, as a place of refuge and safety:

"Lead me to the rock that is higher than I.

For you have been my refuge,

a strong tower against the foe.

I long to dwell in your tent for ever

and take refuge in the shelter of your wings."

(Psalm 61:2-4)

Yet as a symbol, Zion was curiously double-edged. Despite visibly communicating God's presence, it did not exactly offer the comfort of full access. In many ways, it functioned as a colossal "No Entry" sign.

The temple complex was made up of a series of courts, with each one becoming more exclusive the closer to the centre you got. It was the heart of Jewish religious life—but only Jewish men could pass beyond the Women's Court. Then only priests could proceed into the next section. And yet, the Most Holy Place at its heart could only be entered by one man, on one day a year: the high priest on the Day of Atonement (see Leviticus 16 for details). Even then, there was quite

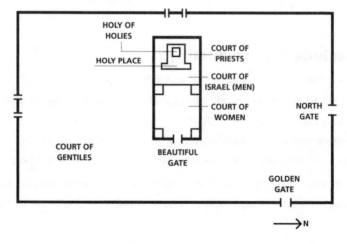

**THE TEMPLE IN JERUSALEM**
from around the time of Jesus
(after Herod's renovations)

the rigmarole to prepare him for the privilege. Everything was designed to communicate a simple truth: sin bars even God's people from God's holy presence. God's gift of the entire sacrificial system was the only way to deal with that.

But for non-Jews, the situation was worse. When Herod put his mark on the building, he added vast courts on either side of the main complex, surrounded by impressive colonnades. These became known as the Court of the **Gentiles**: the location of the moneychangers who so incensed Jesus (see Mark 11:15-17). But it never functioned as the temple proper. Gentiles could not get anywhere near the important parts. They were barred.

No doubt, few Gentiles in the ancient world were especially bothered. Yet it was a terrible predicament, nonetheless. As Paul describes it, they were "alienated from God" (Colossians **1:21**). That is no small matter when that God is the Creator and Lord of everything that exists—the Lord of your life and your death.

Paul has worse in store for them. In addition, he tells them "You were enemies in your minds because of your evil behaviour". The Gentile predicament is not merely an issue of birth; it is an issue of behaviour. Paul's diagnosis is striking though. It does not follow the logic we might have expected. Their evil behaviour does not stem from their enemy mindset. It is precisely the opposite: their hostility to and rejection of God flow directly from the kind of lifestyle they are living.

> Their hostility to and rejection of God flow directly from the kind of lifestyle they are living.

Few have articulated this as candidly as the thinker and writer Aldous Huxley, whose most famous novel is *Brave New World*:

"I had motive for not wanting the world to have meaning; and consequently assumed that it had none, and was able without any difficulty to find satisfying reasons for this assumption ...

For myself the philosophy of meaninglessness was essentially an instrument of liberation, sexual and political."

*(Ends And Means,* page 273)

As Os Guinness observes:

"The philosopher who finds no meaning in the world is not concerned exclusively with a problem in **metaphysics**. He is also concerned to prove that there is no valid reason why he personally should not do as he wants, or why his friends should not seize political power and govern in the way they find most advantageous for themselves."        *(Time for Truth,* page 121)

So for Gentiles, there is a kind of double doom.

- They are excluded because of their race—they are not Abraham's descendants and so forfeit the benefits of God's **covenant** with him, and they follow lives of sinful rebellion against their Maker which reinforce their innate hostility to God.

- They are excluded because of their lifestyles—so whether they realise it or not, they follow lives of sinful rebellion against their Maker.

It is devastating verdict and predicament. And, at one level, it seems so desperately unfair. But who of us can deny its reality when we stand in front of the mirror? Who of us lives with even consistent dependence on God and his ways?

Thankfully, this is not the end of the story!

## Converted—radically

While the focus of **verse 21** was clearly "you"—namely, the Gentile Colossian believers—the subject in **verse 22** is emphatically "he", the God from whom they were alienated. But contrary to all expectations, this same God takes the initiative to overcome the Gentiles' predicament. This is why Paul can locate the devastating diagnosis of **verse 21** in the *past* of these Colossian believers. God has profoundly—and permanently—transformed both their present and their future—all through the breathtaking victory of the cosmic King.

"But now he has reconciled you by Christ's physical body through death to present you holy in his sight, without blemish and free from accusation." (**v 22**)

Reconciliation is one of the most beautiful concepts in human experience but it is also complex. It speaks of the joy of friendship but also the pain of relationship breakdown. Reconciliation can only come about if both sides agree to it, and it always requires humility. It requires the readiness to deal with the causes of that breakdown, and the desire to rebuild. In short, reconciliation is hard.

For all its weaknesses and critics, South Africa's *Truth And Reconciliation Commission* (the TRC) was an astonishing illustration of this. After the terrible years of **apartheid**, the fears of a bloodbath when majority rule eventually came to the republic were all too real. The fact that transition took place peacefully in 1994 is undoubtedly due to the statesmanship of Nelson Mandela in particular, as well as the level-headedness of F. W. de Klerk and others. But the TRC was a crucial mechanism for facing up to the horrors of the past. Individuals could apply for amnesty, but would only receive it if they fully confessed to their crimes and could prove that they were politically motivated. In the end, only ten per cent of those who applied for it received that amnesty—but that went a long way to healing the past's festering wounds.

> Reconciliation is one of the most beautiful concepts in human experience but it is also complex.

However, for humanity to be reconciled with our Creator demands far greater humility and sacrifice. On God's part! It demands the cross. In **verse 18**, Paul pointed to the resurrected Christ—now the focus is on the crucified Christ. Paul's original Greek phrase, translated as

"Christ's physical body", is in fact quite tricky to capture, but the NIV makes a good job of it. It emphasises that this really happened in time and space. Jesus didn't pretend to die. His heart really did stop beating at a moment in history. His sacrifice was real. And just as a representative sacrifice (one death in place of another) was the requirement for Jews to approach God in the temple, so now Christ's death breaks open a way back to God for the whole of humanity. God has intervened and the Gentiles are now welcome through trusting in Christ. That includes the Colossians: "But now he has reconciled *you*".

> Christ's death breaks open a way back to God for the whole of humanity.

This is not to deny the humility necessary to accept one's need of this reconciliation.

A preacher was once accosted by a furious man after a service. "I really don't like the way you keep on talking about the cross so much. In my view, it would be far better to preach Christ's example of love instead." The preacher listened carefully. "Fair enough. So, if I presented him that way, would you be willing to follow him?"

"I certainly would."

"In that case," said the preacher, "let's take the first step. He lived a perfect life. Can you claim that?"

The man was taken aback. "Of course not!"

"Well, in that case, your greatest need surely is not for a teacher, but for a Saviour."

It is not easy to accept that need. But it is surely wisdom.

The results are nothing short of radical. In **verse 22** Paul describes three consequences of Jesus' sacrifice: each describes how we will be on the last day when we are finally ushered into the heavenly throne room. Notice how they are the perfect remedy to humanity's predicament (**v 21**).

- *Holy in his sight:* Holiness at its root is a matter of being different—being set apart for God because we are set apart like God. It is a matter of belonging to him and not the sinful world from which we came.

- *Without blemish:* The old covenant demanded that any sacrifices presented in the temple be pure and without blemish (see Leviticus 22:20-22); that purity then covers over the impurity of the one offering it. So it is with Christ's sacrifice. He is perfect—and he dies for the profoundly imperfect. But as a result, we gain his perfection. Whatever we have done in life, whatever our "evil behaviour", we will stand without any stains at all. What Christ achieves for every believer, he brings to his whole body, the church (see Ephesians 5:25-27).

- *Free from accusation:* This is our new legal status before God. The charge sheet against us, which was getting longer with every new day of our lives, is now blank. Wiped clean. There is nothing on it. We are innocent before God. It is astonishing.

This is nothing less than a total reversal of our natural state. It is quite something to be able to say, "I am *holy*, I am without *blemish*, I am *innocent*". This can never be the result of my achievement or my just deserts. Far from it. It's because of what Christ has done at the cross.

We often forget this point, but it is worth reflecting deeply on it. After the centuries of the old covenant's exclusiveness, the fact that Gentiles are now ushered in and reconciled must give us hope. It means that anyone is welcome. It matters nothing where we live, what skin colour we have, how much we own or owe, what we have done or not done, or how respectable or unimpressive we might be. *None* of that is of ultimate concern to God—for none of it is relevant for who is acceptable to God. All are welcome. Through Christ.

In a wonderful way, that is deeply unfair! It is not what any of us deserves at all. But that is the nature of God's generosity and grace—his undeserved mercy.

Grace is unfair! Thank God for that!

## Conditions—logically

When we worked in East Africa, I remember chuckling for ages at a newspaper advert for a regional African airline. Their strapline proudly declared, "We take you all the way". This was what they touted as their unique selling point, because other airlines, presumably, expect passengers to leave the plane before the end of the flight. It is not a particularly encouraging thought. I would hope that getting me to my ticketed destination was the least they could do for me.

But it occurs to me that it is perhaps a useful strapline for what Christ does for us. He does take us all the way. This helps to explain the conditions that Paul speaks of in Colossians **1:23**. All this is true, "if you continue in your faith, established and firm, and do not move from the hope held out in the gospel".

I must admit that these conditions used to trouble me. After the wonderful confidence-building truths of **verses 21-22**, which highlight how much everything depends on what God has done for us, it can feel as if the next verse shatters the effect. It suddenly appears to depend on us again. Yet, in fact, that is to miss the point entirely.

This is because Paul's argument is not about our *efforts* but our *dependence*. It is about where we place our trust. His words form a sandwich of **tenses**: two instructions that apply now are the bread, while the results of two past tenses are the filling:

- ■ The present: "*Continue in your faith*" and "*do not move*". These verbs appear to be contradictions. But if the Christian life is a journey, they make perfect sense. It is about making progress (continue) along the right trajectory (do not move). This journey is set by the one in whom we have faith: Jesus. He is the one who gets us to the end. This is because...

- ■ The past: "*Established*" and "*firm*". We are on this journey because Jesus started us on it. We certainly couldn't have done that ourselves. But like a tree that has been planted (established) with good roots, we naturally grow up firm and strong.

So do you see the logic? If Jesus both starts us off on the journey and gets us to the end of the journey, then it stands to reason that he is the one to stick with. Don't get distracted or deviate from the pathway or our guide. Who else can we turn to? Paul's conditions here are therefore simply a matter of logic. If we decide partway to shift our allegiance to another, or, even worse, to try to wrest control and credit for the journey back to ourselves, it is inevitable that we will never make it to the end.

That would be like saying to the pilot of that airline when 500 miles out, "Well actually, captain, I'll take it from here now, thank you". And then jumping out of one of the rear exits. Sheer madness!

No—Jesus takes us all the way. So don't shift from him. As we will see, this was a matter of central importance to the Colossian church. Paul has much more to say about it.

But for now, do you see why Paul relishes the chance to proclaim this gospel, and why he is never ashamed to describe himself as its servant (**v 23**)? It is a message that is changing the whole world. We might not know exactly how it is proclaimed to every creature (as opposed to just every person), but what is abundantly clear is that Jesus' lordship stands over

> Jesus is concerned for everything he has made, from galaxies to electrons.

every inch of creation. His work of reconciliation is by no means restricted to humanity, as if we were the only things that mattered in the cosmos. He is concerned for everything that he has made, from galaxies to electrons. But because every race of humanity has its integral place within creation, his cross-shaped victory is therefore of supreme relevance to all.

At the very least, there is no people group or language that should be excluded from hearing it. For now there is no need for *anyone* to be excluded. All can be reconciled to their Creator. So what's stopping us?

## Questions for reflection

1. What has changed in your own life since you first encountered Jesus? What steps do you need to take to remain "established and firm" in your faith?

2. "Holy", "without blemish", "free from accusation" (v 22). How would believing these truths and owning these descriptions for yourself change the way you live and feel about your Christian life?

3. Was this "the gospel that you heard" (v 23)? How do the truths of verses 21-23 feature in the way you think and talk about the gospel?

## PART TWO

# The secret disclosed

## Christ's commission to accept

"Your mission, Jim, should you choose to accept it... As always, should you or any of your I.M. Force be caught or killed, the Secretary will disavow any knowledge of your actions. This tape will self-destruct in five seconds. Good luck, Jim."

I used to love the reruns of the 1960s TV series *Mission: Impossible*, long before it spawned the Tom Cruise movie franchise. There was something spine-chilling about Lalo Schifrin's frenetic soundtrack as well as its tried and tested plot formula. It rarely failed to keep me glued. Of course, Jim always did accept the mission—it wouldn't have been much of an episode if he declined! But it was always a thrill to see how he and the team would scrape through yet again against all the odds. The tougher the odds, the better the episode.

Strange though it sounds, Paul's mission has similarities. Yet it was far tougher—impossible even. Here was this Jewish **rabbi** who had been taught by the best of them: one who knew from the inside how to be a devoted old-covenant believer—until he was confronted by the risen Christ. His life was turned upside down with an inconceivable assignment: to convert the Gentile world, to the God of **Abraham, Isaac and Jacob**. As Jesus said on the Damascus Road:

"I am Jesus, whom you are persecuting ... Now get up and stand on your feet. I have appeared to you to appoint you as a servant and as a witness of what you have seen and will see of me. I will rescue you from your own people and from the Gentiles. I am sending you to them to open their eyes and turn them from darkness to light, and from the power of Satan to God, so that they may receive forgiveness of sins and a place among those who are sanctified by faith in me." (Acts 26:15-18)

This formative experience was clearly at the forefront of Paul's mind when he wrote Colossians. He picks up on several elements of Jesus' words to him as he stood, blind, on the road—especially in this paragraph. Two stand out in particular, which I will take in logical, if not biblical, order.

## Commissioned to serve

In the previous section, Paul said that he has become a servant to proclaim the gospel to every creature (Colossians **1:23**). He now expands on that in our verses. He is the servant of Christ's body, the church—yes, the very body he had ruthlessly sought to destroy until Christ stopped him in his tracks. His point is that Christ is so closely bound up with the church—theologians actually speak of our *union with* Christ—that when the church is persecuted, Christ is persecuted. When the church is at work, Christ is at work (**v 24**). He has already mentioned this point back in verse 18.

But stop for a moment to consider the oddity of this. Commissions often entail privilege—there is work to do, of course, but they often bring great prestige. To be a commissioned officer in the military has traditionally brought that. Alternatively, someone with particular expertise might be asked to join a Presidential Commission (e.g. in the United States) or a Royal Commission (e.g. in the United Kingdom), tasked with a special investigation or inquiry. A member might refer to "serving" on these official bodies, but this does not detract from the respectability of doing so. Membership might actually constitute the pinnacle of someone's professional career.

However, Paul's commission barely brought him any respectability at all. It made him an object of scorn and derision. It was a far cry from his days as an impressive **Pharisee**. He had been brought low. He had become a slave.

But, as he says in **verse 25**, this commission came from God himself. That changed everything. As a Pharisee, he had imagined his ruthless persecution of Christians was in service of God. He now realised how far from God's purpose he was. As Jesus himself regularly taught, God's way is the servant's way.

Paul had no authority of his own. Nor did he have a message of his own. His job was to be faithful to God and his message in its entirety—which is why he was prepared to travel the then-known world in order to "present to [everyone he met] the word of God in its fullness" (**v 25**).

He did so at great personal cost.

## Commissioned to suffer

It is a rather gruesome thought, I realise, but I sometimes wonder what a pathologist might have made of Paul's body *post-mortem*. You will no doubt assume I've probably been watching too much *CSI* and *Waking the Dead*. But it's a serious question: what sort of story would Paul's corpse have told?

It would have revealed a life of incredible hardship (certainly from the second half of it). For starters, there would certainly have been clear evidence of the stoning he endured in Lystra. After the horror ended, his body was dragged out of the city and he was left for dead (Acts 14:19-23). In other words, his assailants had assumed "*job done*"!

Then there were the floggings, the imprisonments, the shipwrecks—including twenty-four hours drifting out at sea—and the starvations (2 Corinthians 11:16-33). Each would have left its physical imprint, which any pathologist would have been able to read like a book.

The obvious question is *why?* Why endure all this hardship? Why would someone put themselves through gruelling adversity again and again and again? Paul's answer is simple. He is

> Why would someone put themselves through gruelling adversity again and again and again?

doing it "for you", Colossians—despite never having met them. He is doing it because it is part and parcel of Christ's commission to preach to the Gentiles. That is why he is glad to do it. More than that, he rejoices in it (Colossians **1:24**).

Now rejoicing in suffering seems at first sight to suggest a serious psychological disorder. But Paul clearly does not take pleasure in the suffering itself, but in its context. He knows that he suffers because it comes with the job. Jesus warned him about that from the very start (see Acts 9:15-16). It is inevitable, because of humanity's innate hostility to God's authority. After all, that is what characterised the Colossians before they accepted the gospel. But Paul wouldn't dream of doing anything else. His suffering is a price worth paying for the joy and honour of his commission from God.

> There will always be opposition to the gospel— despite its undeniable goodness and wonder.

For didn't Jesus make it clear that "no servant is greater than his master, nor is a messenger greater than the one who sent him" (John 13:16)? Jesus suffered for his mission as God's Christ (for example, see Mark 8:31). As Jesus went to the cross, so his followers should likewise take up their cross (Mark 8:34-37). There is no avoiding it. In fact, he said, "You will be hated by all nations because of me" (Matthew 24:9). Nobody enjoys being told they are wrong. Nobody likes to hear that they need rescuing when they think they are doing perfectly fine by themselves, thank you very much. Nobody finds it easy to change direction. So there will always be opposition to the gospel—despite its undeniable goodness and wonder.

But there's another, stranger reason for Paul's rejoicing. It flows straight out of the church being Christ's body. He expects to "fill up in my flesh what is still lacking in regard to Christ's afflictions" (Colossians **1:24**). He is *not* suggesting that believers' sufferings somehow contribute to Christ's loving sacrifice of himself to rescue us. That was fully completed on Good Friday when Jesus cried out, "It is finished" (John 19:30). His resurrection proves it. He truly is the "firstborn from among the dead" (Colossians 1:18), enabling all who follow him to rise with him on the last day.

It may well be the last day that Paul has in mind here, since that will mark the climax of the last days (what the New Testament calls the period between Jesus' first and second comings). This is a fixed term. That means the last-days suffering of Christ's body, the church, is also fixed. It does not last indefinitely. The risen Jesus makes a similar point to the church in Smyrna when he says, "You will suffer persecution for ten days" (Revelation 2:10)—the number ten symbolising a limited period.

So if last-days suffering can be represented by a pie chart, Paul seems to be suggesting that he has a bigger than normal slice of it. But he is fine with that. He rejoices because the more he suffers, then somehow, the less suffering there will be for others to "fill up". It is a strange way of putting it, certainly. Yet it is entirely consistent. He is doing everyone a favour. It is a sign of a truly Christ-like heart, that he is willing to suffer on behalf of others.

Paul's attitude to suffering couldn't be more different from the way most of us naturally think of it. Modern life seems geared towards its avoidance. It has also tended to pour scorn on those who are willing to suffer in this life because of the hope of perfect rest and peace in the next. But that is a calculation that Paul regards as entirely appropriate—and loving. That is because he is a driven man—driven by what is at stake: namely, the welcoming of countless Gentiles into God's family.

As Joni Eareckson Tada so beautifully put it:

"God sometimes permits what he hates to accomplish what he loves." (*The God I Love*, page 308)

## Christ's mystery to disclose

There are some to whom you should never divulge your deepest secrets. Even despite the best of intentions, they will sure enough find themselves divulging them to others: "Oh, have you heard? Mark has got himself into a spot of bother over…" Then once they realise what they've done, there is the sudden but oh-so-smooth backtrack: "By the way, I'm trusting you with this—you mustn't breathe a word of it to anyone. But please pray—pray for Mark to get out of this hole he's in…" But, the secret's out! It's now public knowledge. This is a general principle that all social-media addicts would do well to acknowledge!

But there are other kinds of secret which are only meant to be kept under wraps for a specific period. After that point, those who can't keep a secret work to your advantage! You want the secret to spread far and wide. That is the idea behind big product launches or the next obsessively anticipated installment of a blockbuster movie franchise.

God has had his plans and has kept his secrets. But far from embarrassments to keep hidden, he has simply been waiting for just the right time to announce the launch of his new product to a waiting world. Or rather, the ultimate upgrade to his original product.

For when Christ came, God revealed his "Covenant Version 2.0". This is what the New Testament means by a "mystery". It has nothing to do with the inexplicable or the scary; and everything to do with divine revelation (Colossians **1:26**). The "ages and generations" are the long years of Gentile exclusion, which we have already considered.

But here is the point. Their exclusion was never the result of racist victimisation—as if the creator of all races would ever stoop so low. No—it was always God's intention to bring the Gentiles in. As God first promised, through Abraham and his descendants, "all peoples on earth will be blessed" (Genesis 12:3).

The day this mystery was unveiled was therefore a momentous one because it unveiled God's "glorious riches" (Colossians **1:27**). This is treasure of eternal value and importance. It is so wonderful that it is worth suffering for while playing our part in spreading it. That is our responsibility; the fruit of that ministry is God's.

But what Paul offers at the end of this paragraph is a summary of this treasure more succinct than any tweet, and more momentous than any sound bite. For he summarises the privilege of being a Christian in its entirety in just seven words (both in English and the original Greek). "Christ in you—the hope of glory." They fall neatly and naturally into two parts.

## Our present privilege: Christ in you

Whoever we are, wherever we live, whatever we have done, however often we have done it even—we can still be welcomed into God's family. But more importantly, Christ has taken up residence in *us*. That's right: the cosmic Lord, the firstborn over all creation, the firstborn from among the dead—the one who died for you and me—is present within you, Christian, as you read these words.

> When Christ looks at each of us, he does not simply say, "Mine!" He also says, "Home!"

It was always God's plan to dwell among his people. In fact, that is precisely what one of his names means: *Immanuel* means "God with us". But now, that is not simply a corporate experience, like the temple standing proudly at the centre of King David's city. God in Christ is now up close and personal. He is dwelling *within* us—each of us. Even if we are from a Gentile background.

If this does not help to rescue us from any sense of inferiority or low self-esteem, then I don't know what will. If we are Christians, then God is here with us and in us. And he is not embarrassed about that at all. He does not regard it as demeaning in the slightest. In fact, we might even say that he was longing for "ages and generations" for the moment when it *could* happen.

For when Christ looks at each of us, he does not simply say, "Mine!" He also says, "Home!"

## Our future confidence: the hope of glory

Christ living within us is the foundation of our confidence. He makes the difference between worldly hope and Christian hope.

Worldly hope is wishful thinking—of the sort that hopes for an Aston Martin or an all-expenses-paid tropical holiday at Christmas. It might happen. But knowing my situation (and the state of my family's bank accounts), it is very unlikely. I can dream on… to no avail.

Christian hope is light years from that—it is about confidence. Why? Because it does not depend on me in the slightest. Not one bit of it. It is only because of Christ. How else could I expect to enter God's glorious presence? I need the glorious riches of his revealed gospel. Only Christ can help me there. So I can truly say, he will get me there—because, as we have seen already, he promises to take us all the way.

## Questions for reflection

1. What enabled Paul to persevere and even rejoice in his suffering? Why do we find it difficult to feel the same way?

2. What part does God play in the preaching of the gospel, and what part do his servants play? How should this change how you think about evangelism?

3. "Christ in you, the hope of glory." What excites you about this summary of the gospel message and how we benefit from it?

# 4. THE SLOG OF GOSPEL MINISTRY

"Situations Vacant."

This was how jobs used to be advertised in newspapers and magazines before online recruitment took off.

When work is scarce, employers can expect to be overwhelmed by applications for any job on offer. But when workers are scarce, it is quite a different matter. Businesses must throw in all kinds of enticements: promises of salary increases, professional development, healthcare, office perks and so on.

But suppose Paul was recruiting for his merry band of missionaries. How might an HR consultant suggest he goes about attracting applicants?

For starters, he would be advised to conceal his imprisonment. Paul's incarceration was a direct consequence of his work, after all. As were the stonings and floggings. Then the pay? Well, the less said about that, the better. In fact, Paul seems to think it necessary to earn money in other ways, precisely so that he won't have to burden the people he is sharing the gospel with (see 1 Thessalonians 2:9).

As a job advert in a Situations Vacant column this doesn't sound attractive in the slightest.

So why on earth would anyone do this job? For while Paul might appear to refer specifically to full-time church workers, the job description applies to all who follow Christ, regardless of how we earn a living (see 3:16). Let's look at the job description in detail...

## Job description 1: Christ is the gospel message

These verses follow on directly from Paul's statement of 1:27 about God's mystery being revealed: *Christ in you, the hope of glory*. If Christ is indeed in us, and is our hope of glory, it makes perfect sense that he is the focus of Paul's message. "He is the one we proclaim, admonishing and teaching everyone with all wisdom…" (**v 28**).

It's interesting that Paul can summarise his role like this, since only a few verses before, he assured the Colossians that his job was "to present to you the word of God in its fulness" (v 25). This was intended to reassure them: they had received the whole package. Through his friend Epaphras, they had not been short-changed. But here we see that the fullness of God's word is Christ. We will never be able to plumb the depths of knowing Christ, but God's word will always take us deeper into him.

This is crucial, because in every generation, there are many different "Christs" on offer. Such as:

- The Christ who makes you rich when you sow a seed of faith and donate to one of his preachers.

- Or the Christ who cures sickness when required, but conveniently minds his own business the rest of the time.

- Or the Christ found in "holy places" (which are not even necessarily Christian "holy places" but which bring tranquillity or a sense of belonging), or in "spiritual moments" (such as the "liver shiver" we might get from some amazing music or on making a deep connection with another person).

- Then there are the more political Christs, like the one who is a courageous defender of family values and their upholders (come what may), while there is another who sides with the oppressed poor, regardless of who is doing the oppressing or the behaviour of the oppressed.

There are countless more. Give a moment to consider which are the most prevalent in your culture and church. Each, no doubt, contains elements of the truth, to greater or lesser degrees. But without God's revelation of himself, we can only resort to guesswork about which represents how God wants us to think, act and live.

Of course, God calls individuals to special ministries, and to champion specific causes, but the only way to prevent a "pick'n'mix" approach—whereby we just keep to the aspects of Jesus that we prefer—is to get our foundations right. For that, there is no alternative to the Christ presented in the Scriptures. And ultimately, the focus of our faith is Christ: not a doctrine, not a spirituality, not even a programme of social reform; it is a person. "He is the one we proclaim" (**v 28**). This is not to suggest that any of us manages to grasp Jesus fully—we always tend to obscure or over-emphasise aspects of his nature and work. But that the Scriptures present him sufficiently. They give us everything we need to know about him, and indeed, everything we need to know him personally. That is why we need to keep returning there for our message. *He* is our message.

## Proclaim to all ...

This is true regardless of our audience. Paul's original wording is even more emphatic than the English. Translated literally, he writes, "... admonishing every person and teaching every person ... present every person..." The point is not that he claims to preach to every person alive, but that to every person he encounters, he proclaims not a "what" but a "who"—Jesus Christ.

After what he said in the previous section, it is clear that he has Gentiles in mind. Gentile believers are the ones to whom God's mystery has at last been revealed (v 27). So he now never discriminates against Gentiles in his preaching. There is no elitism in his outreach. This former self-righteous Pharisee has come a long way.

This, of course, does raise the question of whether or not we are discriminatory in our gospel proclamation. Are there people we would rather not associate with? On lifestyle grounds? Or class? Or politics?

Or education? Or race? There is no room for that in Christian mission. *Ever*. This is not to deny that there may be particular groups with whom you or an **evangelist**, or a mission partner, has a special affinity for whatever reason—and thus those people are the focus of a ministry. But that is entirely different from prejudicial discrimination. We can easily use our strategies as an excuse, when, deep down, we simply do not want anything to do with that particular crowd.

### ... at all times ...

Implicit here is the fact that this word about Christ is not just for outsiders—those within the church desperately need Christ too. There is never a point in this life when we will not still need admonishing or teaching. There are no graduates in the Christian life! But it is crucial to appreciate that what we need when we first come to Christ is essentially the same if we have been following him for decades: we still need more of Christ. He is the totality of God's gift to us—and the means of sustaining us.

So Paul the evangelist and Paul the discipler are one in proclaiming Christ, which means doing two things:

- "Admonishing": Literally, this word means to "straighten out thinking". In other words, it is a matter of correcting where somebody has gone wrong. Starting in the right place is never a guarantee of staying on track. Just ask a ship's navigator. Because of all the different forces at work out at sea, a ship's course needs constant adjustment. This is just as true in the Christian life. We constantly need to keep focused on the Jesus who has revealed himself, so that we ensure we are trusting in and leaning on the one "who is". This is one of the most important tasks of church leadership. Even if we are not in leadership ourselves, this is a hallmark of the leadership we need to seek out. Of course, such "straightening out" should never be done in a spirit of pride because none of us can ever grasp Christ fully. We all need others to help us keep on the straight and narrow.

- "Teaching": If the previous task has negative connotations, this is its positive flip-side. It is about presenting truths about God, the world and the way of faith as they have been revealed, of course. But it can never be just that. There will be aspects that stretch minds certainly, but it should always profoundly affect hearts and impact lives. We are not aiming at information transfer but life transformation through encountering Christ.

## ... with all God's wisdom

Teaching about God is a tall order! In fact, left to ourselves, we will find it is impossible. This is why Paul maintains that he does this with "all wisdom". He is not referring to human wisdom or worldly wisdom—as if there were techniques that can be learned to cut corners in this work. No self-help manuals or exorbitantly priced seminars in airport conference centres will provide a fast track. This can only be a work of God.

As Paul prayed for the Colossians back in 1:9, there is a continuous need for filling "with the knowledge of his will through all the wisdom and understanding that the *Spirit gives*".

This must mean rejecting anything that smacks of manipulation or deception, at the very least (see 2 Corinthians 4:2). Faithfulness to the message as it has been revealed is the crucial responsibility of the proclaimer. But the impact on the hearers ultimately rests with God—it is *his* Spirit that brings wisdom and understanding, as eyes are opened and hearts softened.

> It is God's Spirit that brings wisdom and understanding, as eyes are opened and hearts softened.

So the first element of the job advert for Paul's team is clear. Are we willing to proclaim Christ, including all that he is and has done, and all that he promises and will do? Will he be the foundation and heart of your life and message? That is the acid test for Christian ministry. In fact, it is the only thing that ensures a ministry is strictly Christian at all.

Near the end of his life, **John Wesley** commissioned a younger man, Thomas Coke, to help lead **Methodist** believers in the newly independent United States. As he said his final farewells on the dockside, he is reputed to have uttered the immortal words, "Offer them Christ, Thomas." What better send-off could he have given, and what greater privilege could anyone have?

## Job description 2: Christ is the gospel goal

Return to the image of the ship at sea for a moment. The winds may rage and the waves may churn, but the navigator's skill is most evident in the ability to take the elements into account while never losing sight of the final destination. Going slightly off course will not be a problem if it is only temporary and immediately corrected.

That is the pastor's job too—to keep pointing the church to the goal, about which Paul is very clear: "so that we may present everyone fully mature in Christ" (Colossians **1:28**).

He repeats "every person." Just as he doesn't discriminate in who he reaches out to with the gospel, so he doesn't discriminate about who has the potential to be mature. In other words, anyone and everyone can enjoy the wonder of being God's finished article on that last day. Nobody is beyond hope. Each of us can look forward to being everything we were created and rescued to be. Why? Because of those crucial words "in Christ". It is all about trusting what he has done and promises for us. After all, because he rose from the dead, we can be sure that he will present us "holy in his sight, without blemish and free from accusation" (v 22).

Paul sees a direct connection, then, between Christ's presentation of people as holy on the last day and his own presentation of them as "fully mature". There's no magic involved, though: he simply proclaims

Christ, admonishing and teaching. He never loses sight of this end goal though.

This is why he is not deterred when people have setbacks in their faith. We all do. We slip and fall, we make mistakes and take wrong turns. But a good pastor, like a good navigator, is not thrown. He carefully, but firmly, seeks to steer lives towards the ultimate destination. Everyone can be fully mature.

My wife, Rachel, used to be a violin teacher. When we lived in Uganda, she was involved in the early days of Kampala Music School, and taught a number of young people. Since so many were learning instruments, it made sense for the British Associated Board of the Royal Schools of Music to send someone out to examine students at least once a year. The successful candidates would love getting their official embossed certificates when they eventually came. After each candidate's name, the certificate read "was presented for examination by…" At least now they will never be able to forget who taught them!

Suppose that similar certificates are produced in heaven. For those alive in the first century, they might read that each believer was "discipled to maturity by Paul", and simultaneously, "brought to perfection by Christ". In other words, each had been sustained through their lives by what they had learned from the apostle, but; in the end, it was Christ who had formed them into the holy and reconciled child of God he died for.

If you're sharp, you will have spotted a curiosity in how Paul describes our relationship to Christ. He is our goal (as our pastors should constantly remind us, our desire is to be with him) but he is also the means towards that goal (he is the one to present us holy). But it gets even more brain-stretching.

We were told we have the hope of glory, because Christ is in us (v 27). But now we are told that we will be presented fully mature in Christ. Who is in whom? The answer is both are in both! It does not make much logical sense, but it makes total theological sense. It is a way of pointing to our union with Christ—we are so closely bound to him that where he goes we go. Perhaps it will only make sense in eternity.

Which is why the illustration of the Möbius strip might help. Take a thin strip of paper and write "Christ in us" on one side and "Us in Christ" on the other. Twist it once and glue the two ends together. Start drawing a line on one side and keep going—you will soon discover that you eventually join the line at its start. Two sides have become one side—it now goes on for ever. Both elements of our union with Christ are combined and go on for ever. That is how secure we are if we are bound to him.

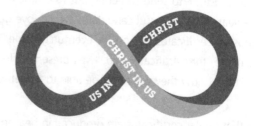

So here is the second element of this job description. This work has an eternal perspective. The last day is our goal, when we present those we have discipled to the one who transforms us. But that means we need patience and perseverance. In fact, we may not actually see the fruit of our labour immediately, if at all during our lifetimes. If you're after a quick fix, the job of discipling people to maturity will not be for you.

## Job description 3: Christ is the gospel means

Perseverance is one of the lost virtues of our time. We admire it, certainly. The achievements of Alistair Brownlee and his younger brother Jonathan, for example, are a case in point. Both are world class triathletes: Alistair won gold at both the London and Rio de Janeiro Olympics, while Jonathan won bronze and silver respectively. But the triathlon is gruelling: swim a mile, cycle twenty-five, and then run six.

The vast majority of us would limit our participation to watching it on TV. That is because so much of contemporary life is designed to save us time, energy, pain, effort.

So we have even more stacked against us when it comes to deciding to serve Christ's gospel.

## We slog ...

This is because it is hard work. Paul pulls no punches. He keeps the goal in sight, and "to this end I strenuously contend" (**v 29**). The word he uses translated "contend" is more normally associated with the ancient Greek Olympics, describing any eagerly fought competition—like ancient wrestling, which was a particularly brutal affair. This word evokes images of sweat and tears, cuts and bruises.

It is not the kind of imagery normally associated with church ministry, especially if your impression is derived from box sets, where the only work that seems to keep church ministers occupied is tidying hymn books. But for Paul, ministry is nothing less than a slog. It requires a steady nerve and triathlete-like perseverance.

But the truth is that God always equips his people for the work he calls them to.

## ... he sustains

Notice what makes this possible. Paul knows that he contends "with all the energy Christ so powerfully works in me". So, he works at gospel proclamation because he knows that God is at work in the world. And because he is working, God is at work.

So the fact that Paul continues, against the odds, is a sure sign of God's involvement. How else would it be possible? What response should we have when the road gets rough, the going gets tough? Lean on God even more closely. Cling to the One who gives us his energy.

But this third element of the job is hardly appealing. The temptation to bypass the slog, to find a quick fix to filling our church buildings or drawing the crowds to outreach events is strong. But it is not the way God works.

So what are the qualifications for any kind of gospel ministry—whether that's full-time paid ministry, or a simply having a conversation with a friend? It is essential to:

- believe that Christ really does have the fulness of God dwell in him;

- trust him to provide all you need to serve him; do not rely on your own strength;

- be prepared to invest primarily in eternity and not in this life.

Notice that these three things are simply the gospel (Jesus) and our response to him (repentance and faith). What a privilege to share in the work of showing people their only hope of glory, and working to bring them to maturity. As bad as the job description sounds, the cost and dangers of such work are surely worth it.

## Questions for reflection

1. What would a stranger coming to your church, or listening to your conversations, say your "gospel" was? What are the alternative gospels that you are most vulnerable to following and proclaiming, rather than Christ in all his fulness?

2. "Admonishing and teaching." How should we admonish each other effectively, recognising we are all weak and sinful? What makes a talk, sermon or Bible study an effective teaching exercise, rather than the simple sharing of knowledge?

3. How can you encourage those who serve you in ministry to fulfil this vision of what gospel ministry is? How can you support and show appreciation for your minister more?

## PART TWO

# The commitment of gospel ministry

## Paul's long-range commitment

One of the privileges of my job is the chance to make deep and lasting friendships with fellow believers around the world. It means hearing first-hand of the joys and challenges they have in following Christ in their contexts. It means that whenever their countries are in the news, I have an immediate connection and always listen in more attentively than I might have done otherwise. Statistics now have faces. That really helps me to pray for them and their country.

So I am always impressed by some of our supporters who receive our monthly newsletter, who seem just as committed to these friends of mine as I am. They have never met them, nor are they ever likely to in this life. They have only read a few names perhaps, but whenever I bump into them, they unfailingly ask after Slavko or Angela, Constantinos or Ramazan. That is what happens when you pray for someone regularly—you grow to love and care for them in spite of the distance.

It was no doubt like this for Paul and the Colossians. Epaphras had been the church-planter, but he had clearly kept his mentor up to speed with their progress. No wonder Paul was so committed to them.

"I want you to know how hard I am contending for you and for those at Laodicea, and for all who have not met me personally."

(**2:1**)

There is that word "contending" again. But how is it possible to wrestle and fight for them at long range?

Of course, in our day, the possibilities of remote connections are almost endless. We barely give a second thought to global video conferencing on a smartphone while we walk down a street, or to transferring huge documents or presentations anywhere in seconds. The best Paul could hope for was an occasional visit in person, but that was impossible now that he was living under house arrest, in all likelihood chained to a soldier (see 4:18, and compare it with Acts 28:30). Failing that, second best was a letter that sped as quickly as its courier could travel (propelled by fair winds or the stamina of four legs or two). And Paul did write to his friends and church contacts frequently. Letters were an integral part of his ministry, not to mention his legacy to us.

But there was a far more powerful way to wrestle for them. The oddity of the image dissolves when it gets fleshed out later in the letter. In describing Epaphras's own love for the Colossians, Paul writes:

"He is always wrestling in prayer for you, that you may stand firm
in all the will of God, mature and fully assured." (Colossians 4:12)

That makes perfect sense now. Anyone who has tried to pray for any length of time knows the battle all too well! But it is more than a matter of prolonged concentration and resisting distraction (though these are certainly part of it). There is a genuine spiritual battle to be fought in the heavenly realms over every individual believer.

There is mystery here, of course. Paul does not unpick the brain-teasers that prayers to a sovereign God for responsible and conscious human actions always provoke. It is enough to know both that unless God is sovereign, then there is no point praying, and that Jesus tells us to pray for all kinds of things, modelling it in his "Lord's prayer".

What is clear is that Epaphras must have learned his prayerful wrestling from Paul—because what he prays for in 4:12 echoes Paul's concerns; and what Paul so strenuously wrestles for in **2:2-3** also throws us back to the letter's opening prayer (1:9).

Some of the believers who understood this wrestling far better than most were the **Puritans**, like Richard Sibbes. He clearly had these verses in mind when he wrote that God "loves that we should wrestle with Him by His promises". He even put it in almost legal terms. We turn his promises into prayer because...

"We have him bound in many promises for all that is needful for us.
We may sue him upon his own bond."

(*Light from Heaven*, page 181)

"Suing God upon his promises" may seem a bizarre turn of phrase,

but it gets right to the heart of faithful prayer. If God has indeed promised something, then it is entirely appropriate that we should hold him
to it. To pray for such things is itself an act of trust. The psalmist was
doing this all the time—see, for example, Psalm 119:38-42, 161-176;
and more subtly in Psalm 85.

As soon as Paul mentions his prayer goals, an unstoppable stream
of logic seems to flow out of him in Colossians **2:2-3**. I have found it
helpful to break it down into a diagram form in order to grasp how it
fits together.

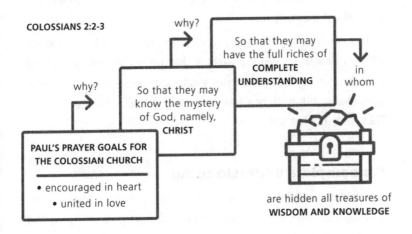

**COLOSSIANS 2:2-3**

why?

So that they may
have the full riches of
**COMPLETE
UNDERSTANDING**

in
whom

why?

So that they may
know the mystery
of God, namely,
**CHRIST**

**PAUL'S PRAYER GOALS FOR
THE COLOSSIAN CHURCH**

• encouraged in heart
• united in love

are hidden all treasures of
**WISDOM AND KNOWLEDGE**

## Strengthened and unified

It's hard to beat this as a goal for a local church. But objectives like
encouragement and unity trip off the tongue so easily that they can
quickly become clichés. So Paul has to *wrestle* in prayer for them. That
is not simply because it is hard to keep praying for people you have
never met, but also because neither encouragement nor unity come
easily. They have to be fought for.

C.S. Lewis once said, "Everyone thinks forgiveness is a lovely idea
until he has something to forgive" (*Mere Christianity*, page 115).
Something similar could be said for unity—it's a lovely idea until we
find something to divide over. That is when loving a brother or sister in

Christ becomes a challenge. Furthermore, the implication is that unity is related to how "encouraged in heart" we might be. This is not the limp idea of generally feeling upbeat; the phrase has the sense of being strengthened and fortified—literally being instilled with courage.

Both of these presumably only come from having deep roots in who Christ is (see 1:15-20) and how we are bound to him (see 1:27). With those strong foundations in place, we are much more likely to overcome our petty jealousies and personality clashes with others in Christ; because all too often, church splits, at their root, are more to do with the sinfulness of one or more of those involved than real disputes about theology.

This is not to say that unity in the truth is irrelevant. Far from it! What is clear from Paul's prayers is that unity can only be derived from the truth of Christ. It creates a victorious circle—the more deeply grounded in the truth of Christ, the more we will be united in love. Then look at what results…

## For complete understanding

Even though spending time with brothers and sisters from other cultures is clearly a privilege, there is always something slightly unsettling too. We are united in Christ—that is our starting point, of course. But I never cease to be amazed by the *differences*, large or small, in our perspective on the world and faith in Christ. Rubbing shoulders with those who are different from me constantly challenges my own thinking and, at its best, sends us all back to the Scriptures to see what they teach. It is thrilling when I am taken deeper into what I thought I already knew, or I even notice something I'd never seen.

> The Christian life was never meant to be lived in isolation from other believers—we need one another.

This is something of what Paul is getting at here—our unity helps us all to explore the full riches of the gospel (**2:2-3**). As with an archaeologist exploring a new area, the treasure has always been there. It's simply a matter of digging for it. Sometimes interacting with other believers is the only thing that spurs us to do this. So do not ignore the value of small-group Bible studies. The Christian life was never meant to be lived in isolation from other believers—we need one another.

## Deeper into Christ

Why bother studying the Bible at all? It's a question we need to return to frequently—especially in churches that take the Bible more seriously than many. This is because we can become so obsessed with theological soundness and even getting the Bible "right". I confess to cringing when I hear talk of "getting Romans under your belt" or "nailing Colossians". The Bible was never given to be the means to competitive soundness, still less a mere resource for theological information. It is meant to transform us—by deepening our knowledge and love for Christ.

Most reading this will undoubtedly have a non-Jewish background—in God's-kingdom terms, we Gentiles are the latecomers to the party. Only with Christ's coming was it revealed that we could be now included as Gentiles. What a privilege. We can know Jesus personally. He is the only reason ultimately for delving into the Scriptures.

## Discovering treasure

In the book *1001 Arabian Nights*, Ali Baba the woodcutter chances upon a secret cave used by a gang of forty thieves. Having overheard the magic password (the famous *"Open, Sesame!"*), he is bowled over by what he discovers inside this otherwise nondescript rock. From floor to ceiling are stacked silks and carpets, coins and jewellery. This discovery sets in motion an amazing sequence of adventures that have been loved ever since.

We don't find stolen goods in Christ. Nor are his treasures primarily material. They are the greatest treasures in creation though: divine wisdom and knowledge. Jesus may not seem much when first en-countered—just an ancient peasant carpenter from an obscure Ro-man province. But he is in fact the "image of the invisible God" (1:15) and the reconciler of all things. He is therefore uniquely qualified to show how life is best lived. He is the embodiment of God's wisdom.

## Paul's long-range concerns

Believe it or not, everything up to this point has been a preamble! Paul has been helping us to relish the vast privileges of being in Christ. That is of course a very good thing in itself. It is always a good thing to do. But in the next verse, we see a darker concern behind it. So the open-ing paragraph of chapter 2 as a whole functions as a hinge between essential Christian foundations and Paul's concern:

"I tell you this so that no one may deceive you by fine-sounding arguments." (**2:4**)

There are those who dispute the value and extent of God's riches to be found in Christ. But they are dangerous precisely because they are not stirring dissent from far outside the church; they are doing it within the Christian community. Their arguments are plausible and "fine-sounding" because they themselves *seem* Christian. They use the right language, have a persuasive manner, and perhaps even have connections with the right people. But it is deceptive. Their words are only superficially Christian, and not *authentically* Christian.

Quite how these deceivers are so convincing remains to be seen—that will be the focus of paragraphs to come. Paul is simply wanting to flag up the danger here. The good news is that they do not yet seem to have made much of a mark in Colossae.

"For though I am absent from you in body, I am present with you in spirit and delight to see how disciplined you are and how firm your faith in Christ is." (**v 5**)

Epaphras has clearly reported back to Paul that the Colossians *are* disciplined and firm in their clinging to Christ. That is excellent, and is not a million miles from what he prays for in **verses 2-3**: for encouragement and unity. The fact that he is so positive about the church in **verse 5** suggests that a specific threat of false teaching has not yet darkened their doors. The issue at stake is how they will fare as the deceptive voices get louder. As Walter Wink put it:

> False teaching is by its nature cruel ... it robs us of the joy and freedom that Christ loves to give.

"The epistle is a vaccination against **heresy**, not an antibiotic for those already afflicted."

(*Naming the Powers,* page 73)

That is a helpful way of putting it because it implies the pastoral care that lies behind a right concern for gospel truth. This is not the spirit of the heresy hunter who is perpetually trying to sniff out the smallest faults in another's beliefs. If a friend is travelling to a malaria-infected area, then it is only right and responsible to advise them to sleep under a mosquito net and take the appropriate preventative medication. So with heresy—for false teaching is by its nature cruel and because, as we will see, falsehoods about Christ erode and destroy any confidence we can have in him. They rob us of the joy and freedom that Christ loves to give. That is devastating if, at the same time, we are having to endure the hostility of the surrounding society as well. So Paul is committed to these Colossian believers—his absence from them in no sense undermines the deep bond he has with them. Because all are united to Christ as members of his church, so Paul is united to the Colossians. The fact that they have never yet met is an irrelevance.

It is absolutely right for each of us to be committed to praying for our local church community. That is a reflection of our love for them— even when they (and we) might be hard to love. In fact, as C.S. Lewis put it:

"Do not waste time bothering whether you 'love' your neighbour; act as if you did. As soon as we do this we find one of the great secrets. When you are behaving as if you loved someone, you will presently come to love him." (*Mere Christianity,* page 131)

This is especially true of prayer.

But we should never restrict our prayers to those we know. So why not commit to praying for believers in a part of the world that interests you, or that features regularly in the news (for all the wrong reasons). Learn more about it—perhaps from agencies that work there, and from resources like *Operation World.* That would truly reflect your grasp of being bound to brothers and sisters all over the world in Christ. You never know where that might lead. You may find you meet people from that place. You may even find yourself serving them in ways that go far beyond long-distance praying!

## Questions for reflection

1. Who and what do you pray for? Are your prayers limited to people you know and the things you see, or are you taking part in God's grander scheme of things: praying for brothers and sisters you know little about in other parts of your country or world? How can you encourage yourself to raise your game in this area?

2. "Encouraged in heart and united in love." Is that a good description of your church fellowship or Bible-study group? What kind of things threaten to tear your unity apart? How can they be combatted, both in your church and in your heart?

3. "Heresy is cruel." Do you have a right concern for truth that is focused on how it robs people of gospel assurance and joy? How can we fight the pull of wrong teaching in ourselves and others?

# 5. ROOTED, NOT DECEIVED

"Authenticity" is the name of the game in politics these days. It doesn't seem to matter what proposals or promises a candidate offers. They simply need to come across as down to earth and genuine: a decent type that you'd be happy to hang out with. Of course, there are always a few that buck the trend, but the winners so often are those that come across well in the media.

Which is where the problem lies: it is impossible to know how authentic the impression of genuineness actually is. As the comedian George Burns once quipped, "Sincerity—if you can fake that, you've got it made". The only way to test someone's authenticity is to get to know them. Only then can you match what you have heard about them (sifting the truth from the fake news) with actually knowing them. This knowledge is a combination of facts (true propositions *about* them) and experience (time *with* them). In fact, this is true for any relationship.

If that is important in human politics, it is absolutely essential when it comes to God. We can't do without either truths or time. Paul is concerned that the Colossian Christians invest in both.

## Stick with the Jesus revealed by God

What happened when these pagan Colossians were first converted? Paul sums it up with what is (for him) quite an unusual phrase: "You received Christ Jesus as Lord" (**v 6**). That phrase has understandably become part of everyday Christian speech, consistent with what we have already seen in this letter about Christ living within us. But it is quite possible that this reflects the more formal words a **convert** might have said at their baptism. In other words, it was a matter of public testimony. In the Roman world, that took considerable courage. It would often have social, political and even fatal consequences—for the world that Paul and the Colossians inhabited was very much *Caesar's* world. He was its lord.

> Why would anyone risk everything like this? The reason is simple: they recognised who Jesus really is.

So why would anyone risk everything like this? The reason is simple: they recognised who Jesus really is.

"Christ Jesus" reminds us that he was a genuine, historical figure who lived in first-century Roman Judaea. That is why he was commonly associated with the town of his childhood, Nazareth. Yet, the more they spent time with him and understood his mission, the more it became apparent to his closest friends that he was no ordinary human being. As Peter famously blurted out in Caesarea Philippi, "You are the **Messiah**" (Mark 8:27-30). In other words, Jesus is the Christ—the anointed king in the tradition set by King David. Jesus really was a descendant of David, which is why he could legitimately inherit his throne. This was good news, since Israel's history after David was dominated by the longing for a Christ who would be as good, if not greater, than David. The vast majority of the kings who occupied David's throne failed in their basic duty of leading Israel to a faithful dependence on God. Peter, like blind Bartimaeus on the roadside (Mark 10:46-48), recognised that the time for this longing for a king like David had at last come.

But this doesn't explain what business a Jewish king has ruling over Gentiles. The clue comes in what was publicly confessed at ancient baptisms: *Christ Jesus is Lord*. It does not just mean he is the boss. It evokes the ancient Jewish title for God—*Adonai,* meaning "Lord"—

used to avoid uttering the name revealed to Moses at the burning bush (which was *Yahweh*). Many translations indicate that this name for God, Yahweh, by using the word "LORD" in capitals. This is God the Creator and Redeemer of the world—as we have already seen him in Colossians 1:15-20. So to receive "Christ Jesus as Lord" is not really about finding true fulfilment by "inviting Jesus into my heart". It is a matter of bowing the knee before our rightful Ruler.

So far, so good. But Paul's concern here is not how the Colossians started. He is confident that Epaphras did a faithful job when they first heard. He says, "So then, just as you received Christ ... continue..." The issue is persevering without drift or distraction or dissatisfaction. That is hard when your life is in danger because of your faith in Christ. Just ask a Christian brother or sister in the Middle East or in parts of Asia or Africa today. They know all too well the realities of what the Colossian Christians were facing.

Yet Paul is particularly worried that they are getting wrong ideas about Jesus: false understandings that could significantly dent their confidence in him. Heresy is like that—it cruelly promises much but delivers little. It is fake news.

How are we to keep going? Paul offers four essential elements.

## 1. Persistently faithful to him

If Jesus is Lord, firstborn over all creation and firstborn from the dead, then there is nowhere else to go. So stick with him. Paul's word in **verse 6**, often translated "live", literally means "walk". We are to continue walking with him and in him. It is about a daily recognition of our need of and dependence on him.

John Stott used to say that we should each "daily bewail our sin and daily adore our Saviour". It is a question of keeping short accounts with him, and of consciously spending time with him. This is sometimes called "practising the presence of God". In fact, Uncle

John (as Dr. Stott was affectionately known) would often start each day with a prayer like this:

*"Good morning, heavenly Father, good morning, Lord Jesus, good morning Holy Spirit. Heavenly Father I worship you as the Creator and Sustainer of the universe. Lord Jesus, I worship you, Saviour and Lord of the world. Holy Spirit, I worship you, Sanctifier of the people of God. Glory to the Father, and to the Son and to the Holy Spirit.*

*"Heavenly Father, I pray that I may live this day in your presence and please you more and more.*

*"Lord Jesus, I pray that this day I may take up my cross and follow you.*

*"Holy Spirit, I pray that this day you will fill me with yourself and cause your fruit to ripen in my life: love, joy, peace, patience, kindness, goodness, faithfulness, gentleness, self-control.*

*"Holy, blessed and glorious Trinity, three persons in one God, have mercy upon me, Amen."*

We could do a lot worse than to start our day like this.

## 2. Deeply grounded in him

Paul was never afraid to mix his **metaphors**—something that no doubt irritates language teachers the world over. Here he seems to confuse trees with tower blocks. He says we continue in Christ by being "rooted and built up in him" (**v 7**). Both images point to how to gain the strength to withstand the likes of storms and earth tremors.

- **"Rooted"**: As I write, Hurricanes Harvey, Irma and Jose have just finished wreaking havoc in the Caribbean. Their devastation was on a terrifying scale. But it is astonishing to see photographs of completely destroyed buildings surrounded by trees that are still standing. That can only come about because of what we cannot see: deep roots. If we apply this to our relationship with Christ, it presumably means knowing him so well that we are not shaken by the storms of misinformation or fake news about him. As with any relationship with someone you love, we will never get enough of him.

■ "*Built up*": Some buildings did resist the hurricanes though. That was often due to the wealth of the owners, which is why poor countries suffer much more in natural disasters. With more financial resources available, careful and robust construction is possible, even to build safely to significant heights. So if putting roots down into Christ is a matter of what is not visible to the observer, being "built up" in Christ is about the visible robustness to stand tall during the storms of life. It is about a willingness to be publicly identified as one of Christ's people (whether in the workplace, neighbourhood, online or at home), and to live a life that bears witness to him.

Whatever being "rooted and built up" in Christ means in practice, it must surely include regular reflection on aspects of his character, his nature, his promises, his activity, his purpose. For all that, we need information—propositions about him; which is where the next element comes in.

## 3. Durably convinced about him

Paul uses the term "faith" in more than one way. Sometimes he simply means "trust". This usage needs an object—you have to have trust *in* something. That is why someone who says, "I wish I had your faith" is spouting nonsense, strictly speaking. It begs for clarification: a follow-up on the lines of "Faith in *what* or *whom*?" But Paul uses the term "faith" here in another way, as a summary of the gospel. This usage has content. That is what we find in **verse 7**: "strengthened in the faith as you were taught".

So we spend time with Christ, practising his presence and trusting that we are united with him. But that is in large part an act of the imagination. Our senses—in particular touch, sight, hearing—are of little help to us. Christ's unstinting presence by his Spirit has to be taken on trust, since we cannot necessarily perceive it. The surrounding culture regards this as absurd and laughable. But it has always been like this. So what is to fuel that imagination? What prevents our faith being a speculative free-for-all? It is the gospel truths that Epaphras taught the Colossians, as he had been taught by Paul.

As far as we are concerned, then, this is the Christ presented in the Scriptures, rather than one of the many Christs on offer in the culture inside or outside the church. The Bible is the ultimate test we have to evaluate and reject religious fake news. The more we know about Christ from there, the more confident we can be in our time spent with him.

## 4. Constantly grateful for him

Paul offers us an acid test of how true to the gospel our beliefs are— and it is, perhaps, surprising. It is whether or not we are characterised by Paul's final element: "overflowing with thankfulness" (**v 7**). Gratitude is a hallmark of genuine faith precisely because the heart of the gospel is God's grace. The opposite of grace is merit—we are given something because we deserve it (like a payment for a job). But grace by its nature is not deserved. The wonder of Jesus is that everything he does for us and gives to us is an outpouring of grace. How can we respond to that?

Here Paul uses another metaphor from the natural world—a river that has burst its banks. The torrents of rainwater are unstoppable and they flow wherever they can. Likewise, the gratitude of those who have received Christ Jesus as Lord knows no bounds. But perhaps that seems unrealistic—especially when life is hard or confusing. No doubt there were dark days in Colossae when persecution loomed large. How could gratitude overflow then? The answer is because of what motivates that gratitude: the privilege and wonder of knowing Christ and his grace.

So when things are difficult there is all the more reason to spend time reflecting on Christ, and perhaps especially on his sacrificial love demonstrated for us on the cross. Our circumstances can never change the reality of his work.

So there we have four elements of sticking with Jesus. Paul now turns to some of the storms that will undermine that. He introduces them with a summary statement of what is at stake.

## Steer clear of the Jesus of human traditions

Call me unenlightened, but I have never been able to get into fishing. If you want to spend hours staring into space in the great outdoors (which I think is a perfectly reasonable thing to do from time to time), then you do not need a fishing rod to do so.

However, I do appreciate that fly fishing is a variation that requires great skill. The strategy is one of pure deception—luring an unsuspecting fish into rising to the surface for the next tasty insect morsel. Once it takes a bite, the hook becomes securely lodged in its mouth while an experienced angler lifts it out of the water. The more convincing the fly, the better it will work. So it is with the fake news of false teaching. If it didn't resemble

> False teaching promises the earth but delivers nothing.

the real thing, people would never be taken in. What resembles good food is a trap. It promises the earth but delivers nothing. It is all surface with little substance. No wonder Paul is concerned that the Colossians "see to it that no one takes you captive through hollow and deceptive philosophy" (**v 8**). The fact that this is the first command of the whole letter underlines its importance.

## Human origins

It is obvious why depending "on human tradition" (**v 8**) is a problem. The gospel of Christ's grace has come from outside—it had to be revealed. Of course human beings have always speculated about God, groping in the dark for what they can figure out. For example, I have on my shelf a collection of essays by various luminaries published in the 1970s called *The God I Want*. It is not a standard work of theology, by any stretch of the imagination. It is more a collection of personal speculations and inner longings. So while some are interesting, all inevitably reveal far more about their writers than they do about God. This is human thought and tradition about theological matters at its most raw.

Paul's original Greek uses a verbal pun that is impossible to translate, so we inevitably miss it. The word for "take captive" (*sylagogōn*, **v 8**) is only a letter or two away from the word for synagogue. It is clear in the next section (v 16-23) that some of the fake news had its origins in forms of Judaism. What is startling is the suggestion that what clearly had its roots in divine revelation, through Abraham and Moses and the like, has now been twisted into something with human and worldly roots. What an irony! Yet it is a salutary warning that this is always possible, and yet another reminder of the need to stick with the Christ revealed in the gospel. After all, he himself contrasted his own teaching and authority in the Sermon on the Mount with that of the teachers of the law (see Matthew 5:27-28, 31-32 for example).

## Spiritual origins

But fake news has even more alarming origins. Unfortunately it is notoriously hard to pin down Paul's word translated as "the elemental spiritual forces of this world", although the options do not affect the overall sense. It could refer to the spiritual battle that always exists behind truth-telling—the result of the determination of Satan's demonic powers to blind and deceive. Or it could refer to the ancient pagan gods believed to protect each country or tribe. Another possibility is the power of prevailing worldviews which sway and influence beliefs. These are the sorts of ideas that lead people to reject the gospel because they think it makes no sense "to people like us" or because Jesus doesn't fit with what is normal in their particular place.

Whichever our view, the upshot is the same. We are in a spiritual battle that goes far beyond the visible and tangible world. The only way to wage it with any hope is to proclaim the gospel and demolish arguments (see 2 Corinthians 10:4-5), and to buttress this with persistent prayer. This is why Paul and Epaphras sweat so much as they contend in prayer for the Colossians (Colossians 2:1). Distinguishing fake news from the good news is nothing less than a matter of spiritual life and death.

## Questions for reflection

1. What is Paul's advice to the Colossians in verses 6-7? Can you sum it up in your own words? How would you explain to a young Christian how they should go about being rooted and built up in Jesus?

2. Would you describe yourself as "overflowing with thankfulness"? What is preventing you? How can you develop your sense of gratitude in all things?

3. What human philosophies and traditions do you think you and your church are particularly vulnerable to believing? How do they tempt us into thinking that Jesus is not enough?

## PART TWO

## Triumphant, not defeated

Advertising, at its heart, is in the insecurity business. That is why it resembles false teaching.

The premise is simple: walk past a billboard featuring an A-list model holding a can of engine oil alluringly, using the latest global stock-market investment app, or drinking a new brand of high-energy sports drink, and the response is guaranteed. "Where have I been all my life? I *need* that *now*." Within seconds, you've scanned the QR code and are counting the hours until you can relish the vast improvement to the speed of your Ford Fiesta, stock values or gym performance. Advertising exposes a supposed gap in your lifestyle while promising satisfaction and wholeness via the new product. Until the next upgrade. Or innovation. Or until you realise that the old version was actually better so you need to go and buy that again.

The false teaching that threatened even these thought-through and thriving believers (remember Paul's praise of them in Colossians 2:5) works similarly. It undermines their sense of security in and through Christ.

## We are secure: inseparable from Christ

There's a classic scene in thrillers. One character gets injured and lies propped up against a warehouse wall. The hero then decides they must hunt down some medical supplies. So, despite her comrade's pleas, she leaves him alone. Meanwhile, the baddies/aliens/killer bees are at large. The tension derives entirely from the common fear we all get when helpless: namely, being left behind.

There are many days when we can feel as if God has done the same. Perhaps he has better things to do with his time? Or we fear we have done something so terrible that we have really blown it with him. The fake news that was floating around Colossae seems to play on those fears, because it suggests that there are things we need to do to ensure we don't actually blow it. We need to keep God on-side, somehow.

So Paul sums up the cosmic vision of chapter one in order to apply it directly to every Christian.

"For in Christ all the fullness of the Deity lives in bodily form, and in Christ you have been brought to fullness." (v 9-10)

Now we begin to understand why the universals earlier in the letter are so crucial. In short, Jesus is fully God as well as fully human. He is not 50% one, 50% the other—he is 100% God, 100% human. That does not make mathematical sense but it makes perfect theological sense. In Jesus, God was living on the earth, in a northern Galilean village, presumably plying his stepfather's trade as a carpenter. This was historical reality. But in no sense does it contradict the Jewish assertion of **monotheism**, famously repeated in Jewish daily prayers in the *Shema Yisrael* ("Hear O Israel…" in Deuteronomy 6:4). "The fullness of the Deity" lives in Christ—he's not a separate deity.

Then, because we have been brought to Christ and are "in Christ", we have his fullness. So there's no need to go elsewhere to meet God, as if there might possibly be some proportion "of the Deity" missing from him. That's absurd. When it comes to encountering God, there is nothing to add. That is why Paul can reassert that Christ "is the head over every power and authority" (Colossians **2:10**).

Paul's point is not simply that we are in God's presence (as if we had been brought in front of him as for an audience with the queen). We are bound and united with him in two ways:

## 1. Circumcised by Christ

Why on earth does Paul suddenly bring up the issue of **circumcision** now (v 11)? It seems very strange indeed. But it does give us a clue about the false teaching (especially after the hint at its links to **synagogues** mentioned earlier); for it is highly likely that some were strongly urging these Gentile converts to be circumcised, so they would conform to the Jewish law. No doubt, they made a point of speaking up for Jesus and his saving work for us—but they probably emphasised that he was a Jewish Messiah and therefore stressed the logic of obedience to the old covenant. After all, it is there in black and white in Genesis 17:1-14: being without circumcision signified being excluded from God's people.

This was a common dilemma in the earliest years of the church. Paul's letter to the Galatians is significantly preoccupied with it, for example. But if Gentiles had been expected to become culturally Jewish in order to follow Jesus, it is almost certain that the gospel would never have spread as rapidly as it did. Christ-following would have remained an obscure Jewish **sect**.

So Paul was insistent that circumcision is entirely unnecessary for Gentiles in Christ. But it was not from a pragmatic desire to make it easier for new converts. It is because "in him you were also circumcised with a circumcision not performed by human hands". This is yet another aspect of Christ doing for us what we could never do for ourselves. It is what happens at the moment of conversion.

Now if some ever accused Paul of being far too radical, of betraying his Jewish heritage, he could easily have turned to various passages in the Scriptures which show that physical circumcision was not in fact God's primary concern. When Moses urges the generation about to enter the promised land to be faithful, he calls on them to "circumcise your hearts, therefore, and do not be stiff-necked any longer" (Deuteronomy 10:16). Even more striking is Jeremiah's distinction between the physically circumcised and those who are faithful to God (whether Jewish or not!).

"'The days are coming,' declares the Lord, 'when I will punish all who are circumcised only in the flesh—Egypt, Judah, Edom, Ammon, Moab and all who live in the wilderness in distant places. For all these nations are really uncircumcised, and even the whole house of Israel is uncircumcised in heart.'" (Jeremiah 9:25-26)

The Old Testament never explained how to circumcise the heart. It is only in Christ that we discover that it is his gospel gift. He makes us fit for, and dedicated to, our heavenly Father. Before he did that, we were unable truly to overcome our sinful nature. Until he circumcised us, our "whole self [was] ruled by the flesh" (Colossians **2:11**). Only he could put that off. But now that he has done it, any ritual circumcision is entirely unnecessary.

Praise our Lord that there is nothing that we can possibly contribute to what Christ has done for us in order to make us more secure or safe. Nothing.

## 2. Buried and raised with Christ

As if Christ's circumcision were not grounds for confidence enough, Paul's second idea takes our union with Christ to a new level entirely. He points the Colossians back to their baptism—not because the ritual itself converts a person, but because it is the public expression of the conversion that has already happened (**v 12**). More than that, in fact, a **full-immersion baptism** illustrates what happens at that conversion perfectly.

When we trust in Jesus, we are united to him, as we have already seen. So follow the logic: where he goes we go. He went to the cross, died, and was placed in Joseph of Arimathea's tomb. Perhaps that seems ridiculous. "I wasn't there! I was born two millennia too late! I'm not dead!" However, "through [our] faith in the working of God" we went with him so that we were indeed "buried with him" through our baptism. Each one of us. But like him, despite the stone and the Roman guards, we did not remain there. We too were "raised with him through [our] faith in the working of God". If that seems unlikely, then remember that nothing could possibly be as unlikely as Christ's resurrection in the first place. That was the ultimate game-changer—nothing seems too far-fetched for God after that. So because God "raised him from the dead", we can be sure that we are united to Christ.

Trying to supplement that union with Jesus with anything, regardless of whether its origins are biblical (as with circumcision), is patently absurd after that. It's trying to one-up God! With something more impressive than a resurrection! And the only events that are conceivably more impressive than that are Jesus' **ascension** and **second coming**.

Some people today consider it arrogance to have confidence in any matters of religion and theology. Look at the wars caused by people who are sure of themselves, we are told—despite the fact that so-called religious wars invariably have complex webs of politics, history and cultural memory behind them; as well as the fact that atheistic ideologies have led to more deaths between 1789 (the French Revolution) and 1989 (the fall of the Berlin Wall) than the rest of history combined. But more than that, we are told that religious belief and confidence are actually incompatible.

That would be true if we were still in the world of human speculation and effort. It is a different matter altogether if two things are true:

- God has revealed himself to us.

- God has saved us for himself.

His initiative changes everything. Once that has happened, then to trust him is not arrogance at all but wisdom. Ironically enough, it is the opposite that is arrogant. Adding to what God has revealed to be enough is pure presumption! We do not need human circumcision after trusting in Christ's crucifixion.

## We are secure: innocent in Christ

Paul now combines both circumcision and resurrection to drive his point home (**v 12**). Our sin left us spiritually dead, and being uncircumcised barred us from God's people, so our only hope comes from God making us alive (**v 13**). But what Jesus gives us is nothing less than a spiritual resurrection.

But how it was possible for God to "qualify [us] to share in the inheritance of his holy people in the kingdom of light" (**v 12**)? We will fail to grasp the wonder of this if we persist in seeing God's grace through the lens of our individualism. Being saved is not simply a matter of *me*, *my* God and *my* forgiveness. Far from it.

Think back to the concept of the *Pax Romana* (Roman peace) from the introduction (page 11). Central to the privileges of being a Roman citizen was the enjoyment of the empire's protection and stability. People no doubt complained about the rough treatment by imperial troops or exploitation by corrupt magistrates and governors. But the propaganda would quickly remind them of how lucky they were that they had good roads, food in the supermarkets and confidence that dawn-raids from marauding tribes beyond the empire's borders would be stopped in their tracks. To be Roman—as citizen and even as subject—was to be safe and secure together. That was the theory, anyway.

The threat to our peace with God comes from rather closer to home. It is internal—our sin, which is our deliberate determination to live without depending on him, our Creator. It is his world—but we claim it as our own. The result is a catalogue of disaster. Each of us leaves a trail of pain, heartache, cruelty and selfishness behind us, however much we might try to patch things up and attempt good deeds when we put our minds to it. Multiply that by the number of people who have ever lived, as well as the seven billion or so living today, and … well, that is quite the catalogue. It is precisely why living together is so hard.

> Each of us leaves a trail of pain, heartache, cruelty and selfishness behind us.

In Paul's day, the Roman Empire could never clear up that kind of mess. In fact, in common with all empires, it was a significant contributor to the carnage. Peace would take something far more radical.

"He forgave us all our sins, having cancelled the charge of our
legal indebtedness, which stood against us and condemned us;
he has taken it away, nailing it to the cross." (**v 13-14**)

Christ was the true innocent. He was not guilty of anything remotely worthy of execution. Which is why he was the perfect representative of those of us who are: the perfect substitute to take our place. The catalogue of disaster that our sin causes hangs over us—until we come to the cross.

In a court of law, defendants have the charges against them read publicly—that enables everyone to know what is at stake. If the verdict is guilty, everyone will then understand the justice of the punishment. As each of us stands before God, this rap sheet is terrifying as well as humiliating. We are silenced by it (see Romans 3:19).

But Jesus "has taken it away" from us (Colossians **2:14**). Just as Pilate's charge sheet was nailed above Jesus' head on the cross—"THIS IS JESUS, THE KING OF THE JEWS" (Matthew 27:37)—Paul tells us that our own charge sheets have also been nailed to the cross. Oh the relief of that! Oh the joy! Did you spot that little world "all" (Colossians **2:13**)? No sin is too great, too dark, too horrendous. All can be removed.

> No sin is too great, too dark, too horrendous. All can be removed.

This is surely one of the greatest reasons for wanting others to know Christ for themselves. We can never do this for anybody else or delegate it to anybody else. Forgiveness does not come simply by virtue of growing up in a Christian home, or going to church regularly, or even living in a supposedly Christian country. It must be personal to be real. Each must come to the foot of the cross and kneel before our Lord. Each must entrust their sins to him. It must be personal.

But that is not the half of Jesus' victory. Paul takes the *Pax Romana* and turns it inside out. He shows how the gospel brings something far greater: *Pax Christiana*. The Romans achieved their peace through military might. Their peace was essentially the absence of war—an uneasy pacification. Christ achieves our peace through public execution as a common criminal, but brings joyful wholeness and harmony;

a community of forgiven and transformed people are as united to him as they are to each other. That is true peace—what the Old Testament calls *shalom*. Just how different these two kinds of peace are is hinted at by Paul's ingenious subversion of Roman power:

> "And having disarmed the powers and authorities, he made a public spectacle of them, triumphing over them by the cross."
>
> (**v 15**)

When the generals who secured the *Pax Romana* were rewarded, they were granted a "military triumph"—a technical term for a victory parade. A triumph was the only reason that anyone could lead an army through Rome's streets. It was a great honour, tainted only by the mandate of a slave who constantly whispered in the general's ear— "You are still only human."

Christ turned that upside down. Paul's ingenious wordplay comes across even in the English use of the word "triumph". If you were a passerby on the hill of Golgotha that first Good Friday, you might have described the events you witnessed in many ways. But "triumph" would never have crossed your mind. "The cross was not the defeat of Christ at the hands of the powers: it was the defeat of the powers at the hands—yes, the bleeding hands—of Christ" (N.T. Wright, *Following Jesus: Biblical Reflections on Discipleship*). By dying and then defeating death in his resurrection, Jesus demonstrates his vast superiority to Rome's might. They threw everything they could at him and still couldn't keep him at bay. Even though it was not immediately obvious, his willing submission to their brutal methods was the very means of his victory.

The poet Edward Shillito captured this brilliantly in his justly famous *Jesus of the Scars*, written soon after the First World War:

*The other gods were strong; but Thou wast weak;*
*They rode, but Thou didst stumble to a throne;*
*But to our wounds only God's wounds can speak,*
*And not a god has wounds, but Thou alone.*

Why is this important? Because *nothing* can possibly defeat Jesus now. He endured the worst the world could throw at him—and still won.

Can we contribute anything to that divine triumph? Can circumcision—or any other religious ritual for that matter—make our forgiveness more sure? *Never!* Because of his death, we are alive and declared *innocent*! And we are bound together and therefore safe. We have true peace: a divine peace which the world cannot truly understand but which binds us together in community. More on that in later chapters. But it is clear: he has done everything we need.

There is nothing to add. Indeed, as is sometimes said, to add to Jesus is to subtract from Jesus. He has done it all.

## Questions for reflection

1. "It is arrogant to believe that we are fully accepted and forgiven". How would you answer from this passage someone who said this to you?

2. What kind of things are we tempted to "add" to faith in Christ in order to give us more assurance? What is the antidote to these claims?

3. What three enemies are destroyed by Jesus' death on the cross (v 13-15)? How has this been achieved?

# 6. ESCAPE THE SHADOWS

The children were quite young when we first moved back to London from East Africa. Naturally we wanted to explore some of the sights and sounds with them. One place we made for was Covent Garden, which is fun despite being a tourist trap. The old city flower market has been transformed into arcades of small shops and is always full of street musicians and other performers. The problem was the human statues. Our then four-year-old daughter was disturbed that one of them appeared to be floating in mid-air. There really was nothing beneath his feet. It couldn't have been a mirror trick because a small dog ran just below him. But when he suddenly moved his arm and winked at her, she completely freaked out. This incident has put our daughter off Covent Garden—and mimes—for life.

The truth, of course, is that it *is* a trick. The performer was draped in a large sheet which concealed a strong raised ledge cleverly constructed to deceive onlookers. He wasn't floating; he wasn't even balancing. He was secure, despite appearances. Even if somebody had come up and offered a stepladder or a stool to stand on, it would have been entirely unnecessary.

With Christ, there is no trick. But there is total security, despite appearances. We saw this in the previous section. The difficulty is that we must take that on trust, rather than from what is tangible or visible. That is especially hard when others come along with stools or steps and offer to prop us up. So Paul has strong words. None of those false props are necessary if we are "in Christ".

The first false prop that concerns Paul is religious activity.

## 1. Don't be judged by legalists

"Therefore do not let anyone judge you by what you eat or drink,
or with regard to a religious festival, a New Moon celebration or
a Sabbath day." (**v 16**)

If Paul's Gentile readers were alarmed by his subversion of the Roman
Empire in the previous section, it the turn of his Jewish readers to be
alarmed. What do each of the elements of verse 16 have in common?
They are all issues touched on in the old covenant. In Moses' law, God
makes very clear stipulations, which you can follow up here:

- *What you eat or drink:* Leviticus 11.

- *A religious festival:* Leviticus 23.

- *A New Moon celebration:* Numbers 10:8-10.

- *A Sabbath day:* Leviticus 23.

In their different ways, each of these were the means for believers
to show their devotion to, and dependence on, their rescuer God. It
proved they were different from their pagan neighbours, for whom
such laws were irrelevant. It couldn't help but set them apart. So in
a sense, the whole point was that people did judge them by these
things! If you didn't follow these rules, people would naturally assume
you were not part of the devout in-crowd.

But now Paul seems to suggest that none of it matters anymore.
Who on earth does he think he is? You can't arbitrarily decide to throw
out what God has revealed, just because you don't like it or because it
makes life harder for those you are trying to bring into God's people.
At least, that is the kind of thing Paul's detractors would have flung at
him. But that is emphatically not what Paul was up to.

"These are a shadow of the things that were to come; the reality,
however, is found in Christ." (Colossians **2:17**)

Shadows have many features. They can intrigue and keep children
entertained for ages, when someone makes animal silhouettes on the
wall using a lamp and contorted hand movements. They can cause

alarm and fear, such as in horror movies when a bad guy's presence looms larger than life. But when it comes to relationships, we rarely think twice: a friend's shadow is far less significant than the person herself. If she is in conversation with you, it would be very odd to keep replying to her silhouette on the ground. It might suggest subservient deference, plain rudeness, or the presence of a disorder like autism. It would definitely not be a sign of friendship.

> Jesus casts a cosmic and historic shadow over all peoples and all times.

Jesus of Nazareth towers above human history. His colossal presence casts a cosmic and historic shadow over all peoples and all times. There is no question that he does this over all that has come since his day. We number our years and centuries after him (albeit inaccurately!). This may well be apocryphal, but the following alleged quote from Napoleon Bonaparte is exactly right:

"I know men and I tell you that Jesus Christ is no mere man. Between him and every other person in the world there is no possible term of comparison. Alexander, Caesar, Charlemagne, and I have founded empires. But on what did we rest the creation of our genius? Upon force. Jesus Christ founded his empire upon love; and at this hour millions would die for him…

"If Socrates would enter the room, we should rise and do him honour. But if Jesus Christ came into the room, we should fall down on our knees and worship him."

The strange thing is that Jesus does not merely cast shadows *after*

**CHRIST TOWERS OVER HUMAN HISTORY**

OLD COVENANT AGE     NEW COVENANT AGE

his life. He also cast shadows *before* it. God was preparing his way throughout Old Testament history. So Paul's argument in no sense undermines the divine origin of these covenant laws. It depends on it. He's simply saying that God never intended these laws to be permanent. They were only designed to express devotion to God until the reality in Christ came. Then once he had come, the "terms and conditions" changed.

That is why, for example, Jesus publicly declared all foods clean (Mark 7:17-23). Dietary restrictions were never intended to prevent an impure life. The human heart is too persistently rebellious to be tamed by food, and so something far more radical is needed. These laws could never be more than identifying marks of belonging to God's community. It seems that by Jesus' day, the Pharisees and others were stretching it all far too far. But Jesus liberates everyone from those intolerable and impossible burdens. They had all passed their sell-by date. Belonging to God is no longer marked by such things. It is instead marked by what we do with his Son. Dietary laws were the shadows; he is the substance.

So Paul urges the Colossians, *Don't be persuaded otherwise. Don't let these plausible teachers make you feel insecure because you don't do what they do. You are already secure, even though they can't see that in outward religious signs! Don't lean on these false teachers' steps or stools when you have Christ. Above all, don't allow yourself to feel insecure!*

The false teachers of Paul's day sadly have their modern counterparts. The technical term for this is "legalism", which insists that our security in Christ depends, in some part, on our obedience to God's Old Testament laws, or to some other man-made code of behaviour or spirituality. Legalism might never be voiced out loud, but its thought patterns still worm their way into our daily experience. We can fear that if we skip a church service or miss out on a quiet time, things will somehow go wrong in our lives. Conversely, we imagine that Christ must be more pleased with us when we tell a non-believing friend that we are his, or we imagine that reading a Christian book (like this one) will earn spiritual brownie points! Take note: going to church, spending time alone with Christ, speaking up about our devotion to him and reading Christian books (like this one) are all good things to do. The problem is that niggling feeling of insecurity, as though these *good things to do* as followers of Christ are *necessary things to do* to keep us in right relationship with Jesus.

It gets even more complicated when these good things are debatable questions of conscience. When it is a question of how to be faithful in the modern world, Christians can often legitimately disagree. Too often, it is a short step from agreeing to disagree, to asserting that those with a different view cannot possibly be Christian. But if our security in Christ is dependent solely on what *he has done for us*, rather than what *we do for him*, this cannot be fair. So Paul is insistent: don't be judged on these terms—and don't judge others on these terms.

The second false prop is harder to detect. If the first entails being charged for not being strict or devout enough, the second is about not being "spiritual" enough.

## 2. Don't Be disqualified by mystics

"Do not let anyone who delights in false humility and the worship of angels disqualify you. Such a person also goes into great detail about what they have seen; they are puffed up with idle notions by their unspiritual mind." (Colossians **2:18**)

At first sight, Paul's command here seems barely relevant. After all, most readers of this book will not even entertain the temptation to worship angels, so the possibility of being spiritually derailed by someone who does seems remote. Yet that is to miss the point. The problem was not that people were directing their worship *to* angelic beings—few true converts to Christ would ever be tempted to worship anyone except God—but that they claimed to worship *alongside* angelic beings. In other words, they were experiencing a profound intimacy with God through their times of worship, and so they argued that those who didn't join in with them were truly missing out. After all, who wouldn't want to worship with the angels?

A clue to how they did this comes in the previous phrase: "anyone who delights in false humility". The suggestion is that these people went through elaborate, self-denying processes (such as extended periods of fasting or extra-long prayer times perhaps) in order to enter into the "right space" for worship. This would somehow give them access to the heavenly realms and participation in the kind of worship described in the book of Revelation. This is a kind of **mystical** experience available only to those dedicated to going through all the right motions.

They had a compelling case because their experiences were clearly special. It was not hard for ordinary believers to be wowed and to feel that their own devotional life was lacklustre by comparison.

Paul's objections were many. For starters, it did those who experienced such things little good at all. In fact, irony of ironies, this special worship of God merely inflated egos and puffed up *unspiritual* minds. According to Paul, it wasn't spiritual at all, but was actually quite worldly.

More significantly, such activities undermined the security of other believers. That charge is serious indeed. But Paul will not budge. Jesus has done enough to reconcile us to God already. Regardless of the experiences a believer does or does not have, the fact remains that we are "in Christ" and Christ is "in us". That status is not earned by us, but granted to us. It is secure.

> The Lord can graciously give his followers special moments, yet they are not the norm.

This is not to say that we should dismiss the possibility of extraordinary spiritual experiences outright. The Lord can very graciously give his followers special moments, perhaps at times of crisis or conversion. Yet they are not the norm—nor something that we should especially strive to experience. Nor should they be the focus of our testimony, because it is rarely helpful to delve into the details of a unique experience. Far better to glory in what God has done in Christ for all.

So just because friends have spiritual experiences and you don't, that is no reason to lose your confidence in the gospel. If you are in Christ, you are already completely secure!

But Paul concludes this section with his most devastating critique of all. Not only were these celestial worshippers not being spiritual, but they were actually losing the right to be called Christian, full stop.

"They have lost connection with the head, from whom the whole body, supported and held together by its ligaments and sinews, grows as God causes it to grow." (**v 19**)

As we have seen in so many different ways throughout this letter, Christ is the be all and end all of the gospel. Without him, there is no gospel. So to charge those who claim to follow Christ, and indeed to be especially devout in following Christ, with losing "connection with the head" is extraordinary. How on earth is this even possible?

*The Bridge on the River Kwai* is indisputably a movie classic. It depicts a fictionalised version of the suffering of British and American prisoners of war held by the Japanese during the Second World War. It won the 1958 Oscar for best picture and the standout performance of Alec Guinness as Lt Col. Nicholson won him the Oscar for best actor. Nicholson is a proud man who initially refuses to submit to the captors' demands that officers do the same manual labour as the men (citing the Geneva Convention).

But as the plot develops, he is shocked and ashamed by how poorly his troops are doing in the forced building of a railway bridge (in the most horrendous of conditions). Seeing a means to improve morale, he decides that they will build the best bridge they can. They will dedicate every thought and effort to demonstrating British ingenuity and effort at its best, despite the fact that the bridge is essential to Japanese war aims. Without spoiling too much of the plot, I can reveal that Nicholson, in the climactic final scene, finally wakes up to the insanity of his passionate obsession. He cries out, "What have I done?"

There are many stories of those who get so fixated by details that they completely lose sight of the bigger picture. They have to be shocked out of their fixation. That is presumably why Paul speaks in such blunt terms here. For all their claims to be worshipping God in intense intimacy, these people are undermining their own dependence on Christ, and that of others. They have lost sight of the big picture of Christ in the details of their own practices. If angels are a focal point today, it is probably not because many claim to worship with them, but because their presence is thought to provide a sense of protection and comfort. In fact there is an entire industry of books, trinkets and artwork that has developed around them. There is no doubt that, according to the Scriptures, heavenly beings exist and serve the purposes of God's kingdom. But it is absurd for them to displace the God they serve in our affections and understanding.

So Paul's logic is entirely consistent with the whole letter. If Christ genuinely is the fullness of God, and he is the focal point of all creation and all eternity, then to construct religious activity which seems to supplement all he has done is absurd. And dangerous. And arrogant. If that seems ridiculous and unlikely, then just consider the countless numbers of churches across the West and beyond which claim to be Christian, but deny his supremacy and uniqueness. "Spirituality" is everywhere in modern culture, and yet it is a fairly hollow buzzword. It means whatever people want it to mean. So there are churches that spend more time investing in mystical practices (perhaps borrowed from eastern spiritualities) as a way of transcending the limitations of their own traditions than they do sitting at Christ's feet in worship and learning. What can start out as a simple interest in those who are different from us (which is generally a good thing) can become a dangerous route to displacing what is of supreme importance.

That this could happen in Colossae, literally just a few years after

Jesus walked the earth, means we should never be surprised that it can happen in our generation. It is a salutary warning for us all.

## Questions for reflection

1.  Which of the two traps mentioned in verses 18-19 do you think you are more in danger of being attracted to?

2.  Read Matthew 5:17-19. How did Jesus understand His relationship to the law?

3.  What would you say to someone who was caught up in either of these false ideas of how to relate properly to God?

## PART TWO

### Relish the freedom

How do you react when you feel that society is going down the drain morally? For that matter, how do you feel when churches simply seem to reflect that culture going down the drain? By contrast, what is the correct response to those who decry the latest moral compromises or get nostalgic for a bygone golden age? To put it more bluntly, how do we get people to be good?

There are two common approaches:

■ *Surrender:* the path of **license**. Whether it is because the things that society gets up to "aren't really that bad", or because trying to resist them is pointless and hopeless, this approach just raises its hands in surrender to the prevailing winds around us. Can't beat 'em? Join 'em!

■ *Prohibit:* the path of legalism. This is the traditional religious response. Essentially it means that we come down harder with our rules and restrictions—we can keep people out of trouble that way. As someone who has worked in local church ministry for many years, I can testify to the attraction of this path. It seems so much easier. Give a set of rules and you can then control these unruly sheep!

But Paul has a radically different approach which avoids both of these options. He makes parallel arguments in several of his letters (most notably in Galatians). But here he is very clear on how useless prohibition is for "restraining sensual indulgence" (**v 23**).

### The incompatibility of legalism

"Since you died with Christ to the elemental spiritual forces of this world, why, as though you still belonged to the world, do you submit to its rules: 'Do not handle! Do not taste! Do not touch!'?" (**v 20-21**)

It is reasonably safe to say that the older and more revered an institution, the more arbitrary, and even silly, its traditions. So in the Houses of Parliament in London, all members are assigned an individual spot to hang their coats and umbrellas. Thankfully, each hook also comes with a ribbon from which to hang their sword. Still. There is apparently at least one Member of Parliament who takes advantage of this helpful provision.

Then there are those traditions that are designed to mark out hierarchies and social divisions. A classic but fairly ludicrous example—all too common in many older British institutions—is the right to walk on an immaculately kept lawn. At my school, this was restricted to a small group of senior students and teachers. I remember being told off for walking on the forbidden patch of grass when young—and so still have a paranoid nervousness of doing the same now. Even when I did earn the privilege of walking on the prefects' lawn, that felt like a huge moment—but it still felt wrong! But that is how conditioning works. After all those years of restrictions, my new-found freedom somehow seemed illegitimate. Yet the only thing holding me back was not the rulebook but my head.

At a far deeper level, the same is true of coming to Christ. He is so counter-cultural, so surprising in his kindness to us, that it can take a lifetime for it to truly sink in. Tragically, the common assumption is that God is a celestial policeman waving a truncheon or taser at delinquent human beings. It runs deep across cultures the world over. So naturally we think that the only way to keep him on side is by sweating at being good. It's all a matter of cancelling out the bad things we do with the good, hoping that we'll get through "on good behaviour". This is the natural religion of humanity. And there is a logic to it. It is all about getting what we deserve.

After all, this is how the world works. "There's no such thing as a free lunch," we are told. Everything comes with a price, even if that price is not financial. In fact, the things we do get for free aren't genuinely free. For sure, Facebook and Google offer their networking or search services to us for free. But we are not actually their customers; we are their raw material. It is the advertisers who are their true customers! So if this is the way the modern world works, it is understandable that we dedicate ourselves to gaining credit: earning our way through life with educational achievements, growing salaries, and bulging address books. We want to prove we have something to offer, to give people a reason to give to us—all so that we can get what we want. It is not a great leap from that mentality to thinking that the same is true of God. Surely, we assume, we just need to gain enough spiritual credit to get into heaven.

Paul is emphatic. No! The wonder of the gospel is that in Christ we are freed from that whole mindset. It is entirely unnecessary. Why? Because we have "died with Christ to the elemental spiritual forces of this world". This suggests that there is a spiritual reason for the appeal of legalism—a darkness at work that blinds people to even the possibility of an alternative to legalism. As we have seen frequently in the letter, we are bound to Christ. We are safe and secure in him. Imagining we must follow all these rules and regulations out of fear of what God might do reveals our lack of trust; we prove we are no longer secure in Christ. It's as if we continue to avoid walking on the grass when all the time the privilege has been granted to us.

But there's another reason for rejecting legalism. Paul hints at it in **verse 20** when he speaks of "elemental spiritual forces of this world" and "belong[ing] to the world".

## The nature of legalism

Just in case the Colossians failed to catch the surprise of his earlier statement about Sabbaths and New Moon festivals (**v 16**), Paul now rams his point home. Even if such rules have their origins in Scripture, legalism twists them into something thoroughly worldly. They are "based on merely human commands and teachings" (**v 22**). They will perish because they are past their sell-by date.

So here's the shock. *It is worldly to be religious!*

This is why religious legalism should be entirely out of place for the Christian believer. We are to enjoy our security and freedom, and not regress back to the old way of thinking.

> So here's the shock. It is worldly to be religious!

But this is hard, precisely because the legalistic mindset runs so deeply within us. Countering it sometimes needs conscious efforts, the deliberate decision to resist the accusing voices of our minds that try to convince us of divine disappointment and thus our spiritual jeopardy. We must stop ourselves. We must say to ourselves, "No! That's just worldliness! God's love for me does not depend on my spiritual and moral performance! It depends on Christ dying for me."

This is a lifelong battle—so we should not be caught by surprise. Legalism is normal and ingrained thinking. But it is emphatically not *Christian* thinking.

## The irony of legalism

Paul then goes on to the most significant, if supremely ironic, aspect of legalism. For all its claims to make the world a better place, it is actually a spectacular failure:

> "Such regulations indeed have an appearance of wisdom, with their self-imposed worship, their false humility and their harsh treatment of the body, but they lack any value in restraining sensual indulgence." (**v 23**)

It is a depressing fact that all leaders have feet of clay—a month doesn't seem to go by without the revelation that some respected Christian leader has been behaving inappropriately or hypocritically. In extreme cases, entire ministries have been ruined. Now, the scandalous exposé is often accompanied by mockery delivered with cruel relish by hostile commentators, which is not always lacking in its own hypocrisy. We are all failures, each with our own skeletons in the cupboard. I suspect that very few of us would bear deep scrutiny of our private lives without something to cause the self-righteous outrage of a Twitter storm. So what can be done? How do we deal with our fallenness and weakness, especially when these still seem to show themselves long after our conversion?

If we imagine that we can control our most sinful impulses and desires by being obsessively religious, and doing so without Christ, then Paul has strong words for us. *It won't work.* These activities "lack any value in restraining sensual indulgence". Observers might greatly respect us (as the people of Jesus' time did the Pharisees). Or they might despise us and assume that we are perfectly insane. Either way, this approach is proved to be utterly pointless. Furthermore, it might seem a perfectly reasonable and spiritually plausible way of understanding the Christian life. But without exclusive and total dependence on what Christ has accomplished for us, religion is useless and not fit for purpose. As one commentator put it, "Any Christless version of truth has no redemptive value" (Robert Wall, *Colossians & Philemon,* page 127). It is not enough for it simply to *sound* plausibly Christian. There must be total and confident dependence on Christ for it to *be* Christian.

**Martin Luther** was a serious monk. If anyone could claim a sufficiently impressive list of spiritual achievements to prove his devotion to God it was Brother Martin. He went on a pilgrimage to Rome to dot every spiritual "i" and cross every spiritual "t". One example of his obsession was his ascent of the Scala Sancta (the "holy" steps) of St John's Lateran. These had supposedly come from Pontius Pilate's palace in Jerusalem, but were brought to Rome in the fourth century because it was thought that Jesus had climbed them during his trials. Consequently, they became of popular focus for mediaeval pilgrims who would climb them step by step on their knees. This is precisely what Luther did in 1510, saying the Lord's Prayer on each step, in the hope that this would somehow release a loved one from **Purgatory**. But when he got to the top, he was plagued with doubts. "Who knows whether this is true?" he wondered. He soon became increasingly convinced of the futility of such acts, whether on behalf of others or for himself. He realised that the only hope we can ever have of being right with God depends on God himself. As he would say in the Heidelberg Disputation of 1518, a foundational event in the early **Reformation**:

"It is certain that man must utterly despair of his own ability before he is prepared to receive the grace of Christ."

This is precisely what makes the gospel so radical and counter-intuitive.

What now? If religious activity cannot change the heart, what can? Are we to throw up our hands in surrender, just resigning ourselves to our inevitable hypocrisy? Well, that is essentially the question left hanging at the end of chapter 2. For our purposes here, we are going to have to wait until Paul faces the issue in the verses to come. For now, we must be content instead to accept this devastating critique of legalism:

- It is incompatible with the grace that Christ brings.

- It is merely worldliness concealed beneath the guise of religious activity.

- It is singularly useless at changing lives and communities.

## Questions for reflection

1. What is so attractive about rule-keeping? Why do you think it is so ingrained in us?

2. What aspects of legalism do you think you have been prone to in your Christian life? What truth about how God relates to us has helped you resist the pull of legalism?

3. What would you say to another Christian who laid out a precise set of expectations for how you should live your life as a believer? Would you be happy to allow them to encourage others to choose that view, or not?

# 7. A NEW ADDRESS

Where are you from? It is the first question on meeting someone who looks, sounds or acts "differently". After all, we think, if they were from these parts, then they wouldn't look/sound/act like *that*.

It was precisely the fact that we clearly did not belong in Uganda that was so good for us. It helped us begin to understand a little more of what it means to be an outsider, and even from an ethnic minority. Of course, as Brits living in a former British colony, that was not completely straightforward or neutral. Being white in Africa is *nothing* like being black in Europe or North America. But we could have no illusions. We could only be guests in the country (a fact too many cross-cultural workers fail to remember)—a privilege in itself.

Our accents, our habits and attitudes, our hobbies and perspectives all told that story. And ultimately, we had foreign passports. If things ever got tricky, we had a home government that would work to protect or even evacuate us.

The parallels with Christian identity are obvious. Paul has been building up to this point in Colossians, laying a theological path in his explanation of what it means to be "in Christ". We often hear of people describing their conversions with words like "I invited Jesus into my heart". This is not the place for an in-depth critique of that phrase, not least because it certainly contains elements of biblical truth. Yet, in the light of Colossians, a more accurate description would be its precise opposite. When we first hear the gospel, Jesus invites us into his heart; when we believe, Jesus accepts us into his heart. For eternity.

What's more, this grounds our entire attitude to life, to others, and to God. In fact, Paul's brief paragraph here can be seen as the foundation for all Christian ethics (the study of morality). It all depends on how we answer the question, "Where are you from?"

Paul opened the letter with a clear answer for the Colossians. As far as he was concerned, they had not one but two addresses:

- in Colossae (1:2): A fairly remote town in the Lycus Valley in the Roman Empire (in what is now Turkey);

- in Christ (1:2): The king who died to reconcile them to God and incorporate them into his life and kingdom.

They may have been born and bred in Colossae. They may have never travelled beyond the neighbouring towns of Laodicea or Hierapolis. They may have lived in a family that blended in with the local culture perfectly for the simple reason that this culture was the only one they had ever known. Yet because they have come to Christ, everything has changed. They have gained a new address and thus a new culture. The result should be that even those who have known them since school days start noticing a difference. They can now say there is something about them that marks them out as "not from these parts".

## 1. Seek after things above

Paul roots this new Christian culture in Christ's gospel journey. After becoming one of us, Christ died on a cross, rose from the dead, and ascended into heaven, where he sits enthroned until his return. Paul's genius is to show how being united to Christ binds us for ever to each of these stages. He just mixes the order up a little, starting with the resurrection and ascension.

**CHRIST DIED**

**CHRIST WAS RAISED**

**CHRIST IS SEATED**

**CHRIST WILL APPEAR**

"Since, then, you have been raised with Christ, set your hearts on things above, where Christ is, seated at the right hand of God."

(**3:1**)

When Jesus rose from the dead, those in Christ rose with him. Where he goes, we go. The extraordinary thing is that because Jesus then ascended to his heavenly throne and sat down, we have too. In Christ, we are in heaven. Already. That is our true home.

It is only natural, therefore, to seek after what Paul literally calls "the above things". This is appropriately open-ended and so cannot be pinned down completely. After all, how can it be possible to put heaven into the words of any language? However, one thing is clear: he cannot mean the furniture or physical treasures of heaven, as if Paul wants us to yearn for material things. That would contradict everything he has been saying. Instead, Paul's phrase must include the things that make the heavenly realms so wonderful, joyful, and magnetic. At the very least, this means the wonder of spending time with Christ, the one we love and adore. That, in turn, includes the blazing moral perfection that derives from God's very presence. In essence, "the above things" are everything that flows from being in the place "where Christ is".

> When Jesus rose from the dead, those in Christ rose with him. Where he goes, we go.

## Unhealthy escapism?

So Paul instructs the Colossians to set their hearts on these things. This means to meditate on them, value them, prioritise them. Above all, let them shape and influence life in the here and now. This is crucial. But is this mere escapism? There are many things about the modern world that leave much to be desired. Perhaps you have particularly suffered because of its injustices and cruelties, or you bear heavy burdens of stress or financial worries that never seem to be relieved. So it is natural to want to escape. We might go to the movies for a temporary feel-good fix. Or we bury our nose in romance fiction that distracts us from our pressing anxieties. But most would agree that constantly doing this is actually unhealthy. It is not living in the real world.

## Earthly irrelevance?

A more subtle concern is the common (if understandable) fear of becoming "so heavenly minded that we are of no earthly good". This sounds like the vague and disorganised child who is always gazing into the middle distance with a mind on other things. His teachers describe him as having his "head in the clouds", because unlike the rest of his peers, he never manages to get to lessons on time or to look left and right when he crosses the road. It's as if he is totally "elsewhere".

Is this what Paul wants for believers? By no means! Think of Jesus' own model for prayer: the Lord's Prayer. We are taught to pray, "Your kingdom come, your will be done, on earth as it is in heaven" (Matthew 6:10). In other words, as the kingdom extends in the here and now in space and time, the beauty and values of heaven become more visible and tangible on earth. A heavenly focus produces an earthly difference. In fact, it should make all the difference in the world.

C.S. Lewis understood this perfectly. The Bible is not advocating a form of escapism or wishful thinking.

"It does not mean that we are to leave the present world as it is. If you read history you will find that the Christians who did most for the present world were just those who thought most of the next. The Apostles themselves, who set on foot the conversion of the Roman Empire, the great men who built up the Middle Ages, the English Evangelicals who abolished the Slave Trade, all left their mark on Earth, precisely because their minds were occupied with Heaven. It is since Christians have largely ceased to think of the other world that they have become so ineffective in this. Aim at Heaven and you will get earth 'thrown in': aim at earth and you will get neither. It seems a strange rule, but something like it can be seen at work in other matters."

(*Mere Christianity*, page 134)

But this is not simply a question of importing heaven's values to the earth. Heaven's perspective changes everything.

## 2. Focus on things above

Paul now turns to Christ's crucifixion as the source of our new identity and address.

"Set your minds on things above, not on earthly things. For you died, and your life is now hidden with Christ in God." (**v 2-3**)

This also echoes something that the Lord Jesus taught in the Sermon on the Mount. He taught his followers not to store up treasures on earth for the simple reason that they will all spoil or fade or be lost. Instead, store up treasure for life after life, "for where your treasure is, there your heart will be also" (Matthew 6:21). Neither Jesus nor Paul is denying that all good things are gifts from God. They are not saying such things are irrelevant, but that they are not ultimate. The good news is that in Christ we have something far better.

It seems the stuff of science fiction for someone to be told "you died", as Paul tells the Colossians here! The mere fact that you are reading these words would suggest otherwise. But it is perfectly logical to have died with Christ if we are united to Christ. We are bound to him. In fact, our lives are "now hidden with Christ". This means we are safe and secure in Christ. Where could possibly be safer?

There is an inspiring story about the preacher John Chrysostom (his nickname literally means "golden-mouthed"), who was hauled up before the Byzantine Empress Eudoxia when he was Archbishop of Constantinople (AD 398-404). She was evidently frustrated by his independence and resistance to her authority. So, in common with powerful people since the dawn of time, she threatened him. First, she tried to scare him with banishment. He replied:

"You cannot banish me, for this world is my Father's house."

*"But I will kill you,"* said the empress.

"No, you cannot, for my life is hid with Christ in God," said John.

*"I will take away your treasures."*

"No, you cannot, for my treasure is in heaven and my heart is there."

*"But I will drive you away from your friends and you will have no one left."*

"No, you cannot, for I have a Friend in heaven from whom you cannot separate me. I defy you, for there is nothing you can do to harm me."

You can't fault John's logic. He does not deny that the various punishments Eudoxia threatens him with are grim or difficult. He simply knows that his belonging to Christ puts them all into perspective.

> We can't see that we are safe with Christ. But we are. We take it on faith.

They are all relativised. They are futile weapons against someone who is secure in Jesus. Down the centuries, this has been infuriating for dictators and kings who have tried to bend Christians to their will. Nothing will work when a believer is fully convinced. The challenge remains, however. We are unlikely to be summoned before an impetuous empress, but how would we fare if faced with such threats? This sort of opposition *does* happen in our generation, such as the 21 **Coptic Christians** captured and then beheaded by ISIS in 2015. Do we share John Chrysostom's convictions? For they are nothing less than what Paul taught the Colossians about our security in Christ.

The wonderful hymn by Charitie Lees Bancroft sums it up perfectly:

> One with my Lord I cannot die,
> My soul is purchased by His blood;
> My life is safe with Christ on high,
> With Christ my Saviour and my God.

("Before the Throne of God Above", Charitie Lees Bancroft)

Of course, we take this on faith. We can't see that we are safe with Christ. But we are. This is not the first time Paul has used the word "hidden" in the letter.

- "The mystery that has been kept hidden for ages and generations, but is now disclosed to the Lord's people" (Colossians 1:26). This mystery is of course the gospel wonder that is summarised as "Christ in you, the hope of glory". It was hidden—but it is now preached around the world.

- "In order that they may know the mystery of God, namely, Christ, in whom are hidden all the treasures of wisdom and knowledge" (2:3). The point is that when we get to know Christ, these treasures are no longer concealed but available to us in all their fullness.

Our lives are hidden with Christ—but the point is that the time is coming when they will be revealed fully.

## 3. Wait for things above

"When Christ, who is your life, appears, then you also will appear with him in glory." (**3:4**)

Because we are in Christ, we know that his return will be a wonderful and **euphoric** day. He will return in his glory and majesty; but when he does so, we will be seen as transformed and perfected. We will appear with him "*in glory*". That seems so hard to visualise. But then it will be unlike any event in the history of the cosmos! That coming glory means the removal of everything that damages or distorts us, that harms or has broken us. All suffering, and all causes of suffering, will be gone for eternity. But there is no fear or doubt here, because our coming glory is not dependent on our sprucing ourselves up or making ourselves worthy in any way. As if that was even possible. No, this glory is brought about by Christ himself, when he returns.

In the meantime, we wait.

There are two types of waiting: rainy-day waiting and house-guest waiting:

- Rainy-day waiting is *passive*. It is like the child who is desperate to kick a ball around in the park but sits unmoved from the front window, desperate for the downpour outside to stop. There is nothing to do but sit there staring out, bored out of your mind.

- House-guest waiting is the exact opposite. If treasured friends are coming to visit, then you rush around the house tidying up and getting everything ready. If there are things (like certain foods or flowers) you know they love, then you will make sure you are fully stocked.

Unsurprisingly, it is the second type of waiting which best fits here. Because Christ has revealed the values and perfection of heaven to us, it is only natural that we want to do everything we can to share those around as part of our preparations for his return. We wait in confidence and security, not anxiety and nervousness. We are in Christ. But we are not passive in our waiting at all.

One of my heroes is Anthony Ashley-Cooper, the 7th Earl of Shaftesbury. He was also known as "the poor man's earl" and is clearly one of the giants that Lewis had in mind in that passage quoted earlier. Shaftesbury possibly did more than any other individual of his time to improve the quality of life for the poorest in Victorian Britain, through his visionary thinking, political wisdom and powerful advocacy. Legislation against the barbaric practice of sending young children up chimneys as sweeps and down mines to dig for coal was one of his great victories. Near the end of his life, he wrote this in his diary:

"I do not think that in the last forty years I have lived one conscious hour that was not influenced by the thought of our Lord's return."

(John Pollock, *Shaftesbury: The Poor Man's Earl,* page 172)

Here was a man who knew where he belonged and what mattered most. He proved that someone who sets his sights on things above will have great earthly impact. Knowing our true spiritual address has a profound impact on our lifestyle and behaviour.

All of this flows from our being united to Christ. We can summarise this journey in another diagram like this.

COLOSSIANS 3 v 1-14

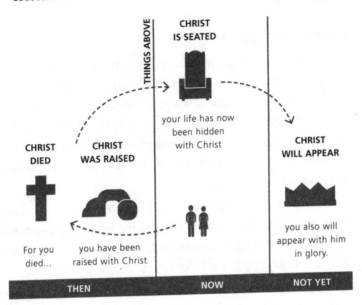

# Questions for reflection

1. What has already happened to believers, and what will happen in the future, according to Paul in these verses?

2. "Set your mind on things above." What do you think this actually looks like in practice? What obstacles are there to practising this "heavenly mindfulness" in your daily life?

3. Write down all the "identities" you possess (nationality, job, relationships, etc.). Honestly, put them in the order they seem most important to you. Where does your identity in Christ sit in the list? Why is that, and how can it be made the highest priority?

## PART TWO

### A new wardrobe

Catch any parent of young children in a more honest moment, and they will tell you that parenting can be largely a matter of bribery and corruption—especially when visitors come to the home or the family is out and about in public. Trying to get youngsters to behave is a constant challenge, and so the temptation to resort to threats of punishment or bribes for good behaviour is strong: the carrot and the stick. It all comes very naturally.

This is hardly surprising since this is in fact how the whole of human society works. We honour those who (on the face of it) make positive contributions to the country; we disgrace those who do wrong. This has been remarkably effective at keeping most people in line.

Christians have the added incentive of trusting that biblical morality offers the best way to live. So when we preach it, we can actually appeal even more deeply to people's self-interest. This is how religion has worked since time began. And if we yank Colossians **3:5-6** out of context, it seems to be how Paul's message works as well. It might be summed up as "Deal with your sinful desires, because God is coming to judge".

But that is not Christianity—nothing like it. For that matter, it is not Paul's message here either; for as he said in chapter 2, religious rules and practices are singularly useless when it comes to "restraining sensual indulgence" (2:23). So what is the difference between those rules and his command in **3:5** to "put to death" such desires? The answer takes us to the very thing that makes Christianity, and indeed all Christian ethics, unique. There quite simply has never been a message like this; for everything in verses 5-14 flows out of the foundation of verses 1-4. They are inextricably linked.

We can see Paul's argument throughout as like a see-saw. He rocks between statements of Christian identity (who we are because of what

Christ has done) and Christian lifestyle (how we should live in the light of what Christ has done).

It is vital to hold the two together—always. We should also bear in mind at any point which side of the see-saw Paul is focused on—while recognising that it will not be long before Paul rocks to the other side.

## Be who you are

Verses 5-14 follow from our union with Christ and the fact that we died with him (**v 3**). Paul obviously contrasts "whatever belongs to [our] earthly nature" (literally the "on-earth things") in **verse 5** with, literally, "the above things" that we are to seek after in **verse 2**. So we can summarise Paul's teaching as "Be who you are". It is not, "Do this, or else".

His language is strong. It is "take no prisoners" talk. But then, if we are united to Christ, isn't it entirely appropriate to behave like him? So Paul says, "Put it to death..." The things that follow have no place here.

The list of five "on-earth things" is dark, although many of our contemporaries might be surprised that Paul picks on these in particular. If asked to identify the vices that most afflict our world, many of us might be tempted to pick up on things like hatred, power abuse and murder. But no, Paul has to pick up on sex! Here we go again—typical Christians! We must understand, however, both that these lists are never exhaustive and that even this list

> We can summarise Paul's teaching as "Be who you are". It is not, "Do this, or else".

is deeply connected to every other heart problem. Paul seems to focus on these because they represent deep and seemingly irresistible forces, and they affect every single one of us. Even if we don't act on them, they truthfully represent our imaginations and desires at their worst.

Some may argue that these behaviours and attitudes can't be so bad if they don't do any harm. Modern people too quickly settle for mutual consent being the only boundary for sexual ethics. But Paul is having none of that. In just five words, he reveals his deep meditation on the problems.

- *Sexual immorality*: This is open-ended and covers all sexual activity outside marriage. What makes it immoral is simply the fact that God has forbidden it. Sex is emphatically *not* a bad thing—God invented it. That means that the Maker's instructions for how it works best ought to carry weight.

- *Impurity*: It is not sex that is dirty (as some theologians down the centuries have thought). It is that sex in the wrong place leaves its mark and makes us unclean before God.

- *Lust*: At its heart, this is pure selfishness. As such, it is the polar opposite of love, which is self-giving. Lust is all about "me, me, me" and my self-gratification, and is not ultimately concerned with the welfare of the object of that lust.

- *Evil desires*: These extend beyond the sexual arena, of course, and entail any moment when I place my own interests and concerns over and above those of anyone else.

- *Greed*: This is a surprise late entry to the list, perhaps! But it is entirely consistent with the others once we see selfishness as the common denominator. So Paul presumably means sexual greed (a voracious lust) as part of this—but it is not exclusive to sex, and certainly refers to financial and material greed, as well as simply eating and drinking too much. It is all about prioritising what I perceive to be my own needs. Paul's killer blow, though, is the description of greed as "idolatry". A failure to trust God as the Provider of all good things, and above all, for all our real needs, is what leads to worshipping other things.

Paul mentions the coming judgment in **verse 6** not as a threat to Christian believers, as if that will motivate the Colossians to reform their ways. It is simply saying that these sins point to what is wrong with the world and why God *must* do something about it. In fact, it is good news that he *will* do something about it. Yet if this grisly list seems only to confirm people's worst fears about what Christians seem to be obsessed with, then simply ask this: what is it like to be the object, and therefore victim, of each item on the list? We go lightly on ourselves when we are the perpe-

> We go lightly on ourselves when we are the perpetrator, but we never do when we are the victim.

trator, but we never do when we are the victim. Surely that reveals everything we need to know.

That is why Paul insists that all of this is incompatible with being a Christian. So we put it to death. That means being ruthlessly self-aware and honest with ourselves. It means identifying the things that cause us to stumble, and then avoiding the situations that make it hard to be like Christ (and if we cannot avoid them, making sure we have friends around us to support us and keep us accountable). It means keeping short accounts with God, by which I mean returning frequently to him in prayer to confess and pray for help.

But here's the point: we do not do this out of fear. Fear is what religion provokes, because of our anxiety about what God might do to us when we fail. We do this out of confidence—we belong to God because we are united to Christ. It is simply a matter of being who we have been saved to be.

One probable image behind this whole passage is that of baptism (which we considered in 2:12). For as long as human society has existed, clothes have carried great significance. They indicate rank, office or qualifications, and so changing one's clothes gives a visible sign of something much bigger happening. In the early church, a new believer would take off old clothes before being fully immersed in water (representing dying and rising with Christ). Then he or she would put on new, clean clothes (representing what they had become in Christ). So

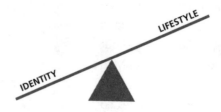

the attitudes and lifestyles that Paul points to here are from the old way of life (**3:7**)—but we have "taken off [our] old self with its practices and have put on the new self" (**v 9-10**).

Of course, what goes on in a person's heart is invisible to others (thankfully). Instead, the first outworking of a person's internal life is their language. Jesus alluded to this when discussing what makes someone unclean. It is not food that goes into the mouth, but the words that pour out, having originated in the heart (Mark 7:20-23). That is presumably why Paul moves on to a list of verbal sins in Colossians **3:8**:

- anger

- rage

- malice

- slander

- filthy language

The human mouth is like one of those effluent pipes that can still be found in many parts of the world. All the refuse and sewage from a town is brought together and pumped untreated out to sea, as if that will make the problem just go away. But the consequences of this pollution can be devastating and far-reaching. Cruel or malignant words are like that effluent. We might dismiss their weight with crass lines like "I didn't really mean it" or "I was only joking". But our words have revealed total disrespect for the person to whom or about whom we are talking.

Again, if we don't grasp the seriousness of this list (perhaps because we excuse so much in ourselves), just consider what it is like to be on the receiving end of these kinds of words.

It is no accident, then, that Paul concludes this grim litany with a plea for truth-telling. But notice his argument. There is no "or else". He is still on his ethics see-saw. It is about living up to the person we became when we came to Christ, when we "[took] off the old self" and "put on the new self" (**v 9-10**).

But if this seems too hard, remember: God is the One at work. He is the one who is renewing our self "in knowledge in the image of its Creator". It is very striking. Paul hasn't laid down any rules. He simply says we need to become more like Jesus, our Saviour and Creator.

## Love who you belong to

The proof of the pudding is in the eating, they say. And the proof of the Christian's conversion is in our interactions with others. It is almost impossible to grow as a disciple in isolation. But the church fellowship is not simply other people who are like us. The church was never designed to be a club for like-minded or same-cultured people. The whole point of the church is it that it brings people who are *different* together in one new group. This is why Paul reminds readers of the wonder of Christ's reconciling work over every single human division:

"Here there is no Gentile or Jew, circumcised or uncircumcised, barbarian, **Scythian**, slave or free, but Christ is all, and is in all."

(**v 11**)

In my work, I have had the privilege of spending time with people who, humanly speaking, should not meet in the same room together, let alone belong to the same community. I have preached in a small fellowship in Istanbul which is led by three elders: one Turk, one Armenian and one Kurd. If you know anything about the history of the region, you will know how extraordinary that is. Or there was the prayer meeting I attended in Croatia, only a decade or so after the end of the Balkan War. The organisers called on a Serb, a Bosnian and a Croat to lead us in prayer for the countries of former Yugoslavia, with each one calling on God to bless one of the *other* countries. These have been wonderful glimpses into what a truly global, *reconciled* church of God looks like. Or to be more accurate, it is a glimpse of what the global church of God actually *is*.

Here is the identity side of the see-saw again. This is what we are together! It is all of God. Just look at what he has already done (**v 12**). We are his:

- *chosen people:* This is no accident. Like the schoolchild who is bullied for being adopted, we can echo with her, "Your parents had to have you; my parents chose me!"

- *holy people*: In other words, we are set apart for God and we belong to God. Being holy is our status before him.

- *dearly loved people*: This is the most remarkable of all. Is there any other worldview or religion that convinces its followers of being loved? Of course, there are times in life when we do not feel loved. Yet that is hardly relevant when compared to the fact of being loved; for God proved it in an unequivocal act—at the cross.

Jesus is frustratingly unfussy about who he chooses and loves. He does not discriminate, which is why it is worse than a tragedy when Christians do. It suggests we think we are somehow superior to some of those for whom Christ died—as if we were more deserving, some-how, when the truth is that none of us deserves for it to be this good.

> Jesus is frustratingly unfussy about who he chooses and loves. He does not discriminate.

So in the light of these glorious truths, Paul says, *Live it out!* But he has no illusions. It will be hard. It requires an act of will, like putting on new clothes after baptism—a deliberate decision to wear "compassion, kindness, humility, gentleness and patience". There is no sentimentality here. Each of these can feel like a very tall order, especially when we are tired, or over-stretched, or simply struggling with life. None of us gets this right. But there is no "or else" in Paul's argument. Only "because you are". These five virtues perfectly describe Jesus in his relationships. They are precisely the things that made him so magnetic and attractive. People wanted to be with him, especially the lowlifes, the outcasts, and the "sinners" and tax collectors. If you don't believe that, just reflect on how much you would prefer others to treat you with compassionate kindness and gentle patience, instead of expletive-filled rage and malicious cruelty. It's a no-brainer.

But this is the opposite of how many regard Christianity today. Too many think church is for religious people, and not moral failures. So they assume Jesus is not for them, and stay away. We can hardly be said to be like Jesus if that happens, because the moral failures of Jesus' day flocked to him, while the religious people had him killed. How different our witness as a community would be if our community life really was different from that of the world around. Paul sums up with three profound challenges in **verses 13-14**.

## Bear with one another

The word in **verse 12** for patience literally means big-hearted—and there are always going to be members of the community who require from us very big hearts if we are to put up with them. (Remember that we ourselves will make similar demands on others!) This is an act of will. It is part of our new clothes.

## Forgive one another

As we considered back in 2:3, forgiveness never comes naturally (see page 79). But a Christian community is only going to survive if *everyone* is dishing out forgiveness left, right and centre. That includes the pastor and leaders being willing to forgive the congregation ... and vice versa. It includes the old being willing to forgive the young ... and vice versa. It includes the well-to-do and respectable being willing to forgive the "not so…" and vice versa. Of course, some situations are highly complicated, and they might even require professional mediation and support. We should not be naive about this. But it does all depend on an attitude: the willingness to forgive. This is an act of will. It is part of our new clothes.

But notice—we do this not "or else", but "because God…". We forgive because we have been forgiven (**3:13**).

## Love one another

Again, there is no sentimentality here. This is not the kind of love that can be expressed in a cheap greetings card. It can involve great heartache and energy. It will always bring a cost. But it will keep a community of different and seemingly incompatible people together. And that is what will make the world sit up and say, "There is something different about these people".

So the next time you are tempted to complain about the music team at church, or the quality of sermons, or the rebelliousness of the youth group, or whatever it might be—stop yourself. Prayerfully, remove your "on-earth" clothes and replace them with the "from-above" clothes. And be who you are so that you love who you belong to. This is an act of will.

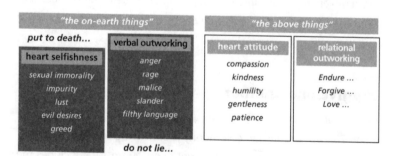

| "the on-earth things" | | "the above things" | |
|---|---|---|---|
| **put to death...** | **verbal outworking** | **heart attitude** | **relational outworking** |
| **heart selfishness** | anger | compassion | |
| sexual immorality | rage | kindness | Endure ... |
| impurity | malice | humility | Forgive ... |
| lust | slander | gentleness | Love ... |
| evil desires | filthy language | patience | |
| greed | | | |
| | **do not lie...** | | |

# Questions for reflection

1. Which of the sins outlined in verses 5-9 are particular issues for you? Which of the virtues require most effort? Make a list and determine to make a prayerful concerted effort with these things in the next week.

2. "Christ is all, and is in all." How can we subtly continue to discriminate against other people? What is the antidote to any ingrained racism, class-ism or other kinds of discrimination we may harbour in our hearts?

3. Endure, forgive, love... Which of these do people find hardest to do in your fellowship? Why is it so corrosive to a church's life and witness when these things are not practised?

# 8. REDEEMED COMMUNITY LIFE

Christianity is all about grace. I have lost count of the number of sermons I have heard that proclaim that. And don't get me wrong. That is a good thing, and as it should be. But it often leaves me with a lurking fear. "You proclaim that, but does it work like that?" Will it actually be more a matter of "saved by grace, continue by works"?

Paul has gone to great length to explain that religion is useless at dealing with sin's destructive passions. He insists we have been freed from rules. But how on earth are we going to live together? We will have to have some rules, surely. In short, how does a legalism-free community survive?

The rest of Colossians 3 answers this. It also proves why the church can never be like a country, because states need rulers, legislation and enforcement. It's simply not possible to make laws about the kinds of things that Paul advocates. After all, how do you police whether someone has been sufficiently compassionate, kind or patient (3:12) or if Christ's message has reached an acceptable level of rich indwelling (**v 16**) in a home group? We are a long way from legalism here, which is why Paul constantly proposes values and characteristics, and not measurable things like rules and punishments. But this is entirely consistent with the idea of the gospel being God's gift.

In one of his books, Tim Keller describes meeting a woman who joined Redeemer, the church he used to lead in New York City. She had been taken to church as a child but had since assumed that we make ourselves acceptable to God by being good enough. Then, when she first encountered the gospel at Redeemer, everything changed. But if anything, she initially found it more scary, not less, which naturally provoked Keller to ask why. Her answer was fascinating:

"If I was saved by my good works then there would be a limit to what God could ask of me or put me through. I would be like a taxpayer with 'rights'—I would have done my duty and now I would deserve a certain quality of life. But if I am a sinner saved by sheer grace—then there's nothing he cannot ask of me…"

Keller makes a crucial observation here:

"She understood the dynamic of grace and gratitude. If when you have lost all fear of punishment you also lose all incentive to live a good, unselfish life, then the only incentive you ever had to live a decent life was fear. This woman could see immediately that the wonderful-beyond-belief teaching of salvation by sheer grace had an edge to it. She knew that if she was a sinner saved by grace, she was (if anything) more subject to the sovereign Lordship of God. She knew that if Jesus really had done all this for her, she would not be her own. She would joyfully, gratefully belong to Jesus, who provided all this for her at infinite cost to himself."

(*The Reason for God,* page 182)

From the outside that might sound coercive, like a grinding obligation. From the inside the motivation is all joy.

Having seen that 3:1-4 is the foundation for all Christian ethics, it should be no surprise, then, that the key word in this section is gratitude. It comes in each of the three verses (**v 15, 16, 17**). What alternative response is even possible? But that gift of Christ's grace changes us, because Christ's grace changes everything. We see that in three key ways.

## 1. Thankful for the peace of Christ

In a Christian community, we are not shaped by rules, but we are shaped by a Ruler. The whole of Colossians has been founded on the truth that Christ is the cosmic King. But his rule is unlike any other. It is a rule of peace. Yet isn't that what the Roman Empire claimed? *Be loyal to Lord Caesar, and he will protect you and make you prosper.* Your children can grow up in safety under our benign command. This was the way of the *Pax Romana*. How different it is from the *Pax Christiana*.

> We are not shaped by rules ... we are shaped by a Ruler.

"Let the peace of Christ rule in your hearts,
  since as members of one body you were called to peace." (**v 15**)

Jesus promised to give his followers peace, "not ... as the world gives" (John 14:27) but peace to be found in him, even in the face of trouble that the world gives (John 16:33). This is a deep contentment unmoved by the life-storms that buffet us and shake our faith. It is an internal confidence.

But while this is a glorious truth, it is not in fact what Paul is referring to. His concern here is the constant challenge for Christians to live together. We have been brought together into one body by Christ's reconciling work. That is a given. He has bound us in peace, as Paul says in Colossians 3:14. But behaving as if we are one body is most definitely not a given. Peace in the church never comes naturally, and so demands constant attention and effort. But how? Through the peace of Christ.

Conflict will always arise when two or more people are together. There are many reasons: some neutral (like basic misunderstanding), some negative (like selfishness or hidden agendas), and some that might even be positive (like both wanting the best for a situation but having differing routes to achieving it). So conflict among believers is not by itself the problem, but the way it gets handled can be. The key in Paul's mind here seems to be Christ's peace ruling "in your hearts". This is not super-spiritual escapism, as if we simply need to meditate on Jesus and feel peaceful before an argument. Since the heart is the source of all those passions and lusts which cause so many problems in the world, and which Paul referred to in verses

5-9, he is saying Christ must rule there. The peace he achieved on the cross to reconcile us to God and to each other must be what commentator Douglas Moo calls "the decisive factor" in any dispute.

Paul will not give us rules. He simply urges us to be wise. Stop and consider what difference Christ's peace makes in any given situation. This will surely force us to face up to any selfishness on our part, at the very least. Of course, resolving conflicts may require help from mediating third parties. Sometimes that can be a pastor. At other times it may need to be someone outside the fellowship, especially if the conflict involves those in leadership. Paul himself mediated for those in Philippi (Philippians 4:2-3). How can those who have been reconciled to their heavenly Father through the death of his cosmic King remain unreconciled to their brothers and sisters?

Some time ago, I heard about a church fellowship in East Africa. In common with churches around the world that use **liturgy** during services, they would always have a moment to prepare for the Lord's Supper by "sharing Christ's peace". In many denominations the liturgy is actually based on this very verse (Colossians **3:15**), but what happens next varies quite wildly. For those who are more repressed like me with my English culture, there is usually an awkward pause when people reluctantly raise an eyebrow to one another or even offer a handshake. In warmer contexts, there might be hugs, chatter and raucous laughter.

But in this particular church, the minister announced the Peace with startling words. He mentioned the deep divisions over a dispute that had provoked some very nasty infighting. Because Christ had made the opponents all one body, he was going to stop the service until they had faced up to the wounds they had caused and had reconciled with one another. The original dispute was not the issue. What mattered was the way they had treated each other. Since the dispute was so complex, they actually had to abandon the service until the following Sunday, before matters were sufficiently resolved for the Lord's Supper to be resumed! That is quite an extreme, but evidently necessary, step. What is clear, however, is that the minister well understood what Paul wrote here. Do we take our community life as seriously as this African brother did?

> Stop and consider what difference Christ's peace makes in any given situation.

Note how Paul slips in the words "and be thankful". It seems to be an afterthought—but it is actually essential. The mindset of gratitude has been one of the letter's consistent themes (look back to 1:12 and 2:7). It is wholly appropriate here. If every individual involved in a church dispute insisted on returning to what he or she was thankful to God for, it would guarantee that the relationships would be profoundly improve. It would put our identity in Christ centre stage—and thereby make it more likely that people would bear with and forgive one another (3:13).

## 2. Thankful for the message of Christ

The centrality of Jesus to this letter is reinforced by Paul's unusual phrase "the message of Christ" (literally "the word of Christ") in **verse 16**. Far more common in Scripture is the phrase "the word of God". But Christ is constantly the centre of everything in a Christian community, just as he is the Lord of the cosmos.

It is probable that Paul is not referring here to the words that Jesus himself taught (as found in the Gospels), although they are obviously included. Instead he has in view the whole package of teaching about Christ: the message that Paul has consistently preached and which Epaphras proclaimed in Colossae. But this is no abstract doctrine—it is the story into which Paul's readers have been swept up (as illustrated by the diagram at the end of the previous chapter—see page 136). The gospel of being bound to Christ is what is to "dwell among [us] richly", because it is to inform every aspect of our lives. But how is this to happen?

## Teaching the message of Christ

The words "teach and admonish one another" should seem familiar. Back in 1:28, Paul explained that "admonishing and teaching everyone with all wisdom, so that we may present everyone fully mature in Christ" was the priority for him and his fellow evangelists. Now Paul says this is what the Colossians are to do with the message of Christ. But notice how, yet again, Paul omits any mention of leaders at this point (just as he did not mention them in the letter's opening greeting in 1:2). Contrary to expectations, this is not a job for leaders—but for believers! This is therefore not only a matter of what is said from the pulpit, or in home groups, or baptism classes. Teaching and challenging from Christ's word is not a job just for Christians in paid ministry but for all believers. If Christ is your Lord, then his word is your treasure. His message shapes and directs all conversations and relationships between all members of his church.

Of course, this needs great wisdom, as Paul says. It is not about quoting a verse at someone. It is a matter of understanding the whole message of Christ, and helping a brother or sister see their place within it. If admonishing (literally "warning") is genuinely necessary, great care is also necessary. Whatever is said must be clothed with "compassion, kindness, humility, gentleness and patience" (3:12). Not even pastors get that right all the time. What is clear though is that it needs to be motivated by sincere gratitude (as Paul repeats at the end of **verse 16**) and a deep and personal dependence on God's grace in Christ. None of us are exempted from needing that. Someone once beautifully defined evangelism as "one beggar showing another beggar where to find food". The same could be said of the place of teaching in church life.

Paul's application of this will surprise some.

## Singing the message of Christ

Teaching comes "through psalms, hymns, and songs from the Spirit", and in "singing to God with gratitude in your hearts". Paul is not suggesting that this is the only or even primary means of teaching. But he is saying that what we sing is fundamental to what we teach and learn.

> Teaching and challenging from Christ's word is a job for all believers.

My old boss used to joke that church disputes very often boil down to music and flowers! While who does what on the flowers rota (if you have one) may affect only a handful of people, there is something about music that tends to bring out the worst in everyone. People fight about musical style and tempo, instrumentation and poetry. Things can get heated so fast. What a tragedy.

Even though Paul could never have anticipated all the debates and disputes that would come long after him, **verse 16** is wonderfully nuanced:

- *"Teaching and admonishing":* This may seem like an incongruous motivation for our singing. But how often do we come out of a church service singing a sermon? Good preaching can and does impact us and bring the word richly into our lives. But a good sing can do that even more memorably! So it is vital that our songs have words that rejoice in gospel truths faithfully.

- *"Psalms, hymns and, songs":* Even at this early stage in church history, it seems there was a variety in singing. It is unlikely there were absolute distinctions between the types of singing in mind. So it seems reasonable to assume that they sang a combination of scriptural songs (the Old Testament psalms) and contemporary compositions (for example, the *Servant Song* of Philippians 2:5-11 perhaps).

- *"Singing to God with gratitude":* These songs are not just horizontal (teaching one another) but they are also clearly vertical (directed to God). We are indeed worshipping God (literally, declaring his true worth). There is an unfortunate discussion in some churches that seems to have reached an absurd extremity whereby what we do in our church meetings is considered to be only preparing us for worship (see Colossians **3:17**) rather than engaging *in* worship. How absurd. If songs and psalms being sung *to* God are not part of our worship, then it is hard to know what worship is.

## 3. Thankful for the name of Christ

The word "whatever" seems to have become something of a teenage mantra. As a response to a teacher's rebuke or parent's challenge, it brilliantly conveys an air of effortless aloofness and casual rebellion.

But the word needs redeeming. It is a wonderfully open-ended word, which is why Paul uses it here. For that reason, it is a word that legalists hate. They want their rules clearly defined to ensure they are clearly kept or broken, and thus easily patrolled. But a lifestyle shaped by grace can never be like that. There are no checklists in a grace mindset. Instead, at its centre is the person of Christ—or to be more specific here, his name.

"And whatever you do, whether in word or deed, do it all in the name of the Lord Jesus, giving thanks to God the Father through him." (**v 17**)

Acting in someone's name means both representing that person and acting with their authority. So doing *everything* in Christ's name is no small claim. If Christians stopped for a moment to consider what Jesus might actually think, let alone do, about what they do in his name, would they persist in doing it? Perhaps a test of this could be to imagine this action or that conversation being included in Jesus' story in the Gospels. Would it seem out of place or entirely consistent? Would it proclaim the grace and kindness that Jesus so wonderfully displays?

> Acting in someone's name means both representing that person and acting with their authority.

Some commentators have reduced this verse to corporate church life, as if what Paul had in mind was just our services and meetings. Therefore "word or deed" is shrunk down to sermons and sacraments (baptism and communion). But that cannot be right. When Paul says "whatever", he really means whatever. This is about the whole of life. All of it is to be worship—living for Christ the King by speaking and acting in the name of Christ the King. And gratitude to God our Father through what he has done is the acid test. Gratitude again and again brings us back to this simple truth: we are not "taxpayers with rights" but sinners saved by grace.

## Questions for reflection

1. What are the three ingredients for a healthy Christian life (v 15, 16, 17)? How do you think you match up to these criteria? What about your church?

2. "Saved by grace, continue by works." Where do you see this error creeping into your own thinking? Think of some concrete examples of where it creeps into church life and the expectations we place on each other as believers.

3. How do you think about singing? How does the insight in this passage—about singing being a big (if not major) part of the way we are taught and admonished—help you think differently about the music at your church?

## PART TWO

### Redeemed family life

"Whatever you do…" (**v 17**). Where better than your home to test and prove that dedication to Christ's service really does embrace everything? Paul would have been confused by the modern idea that we can divorce private life from public life, as if Jesus is only concerned with one or the other. As we saw in chapter 2, Abraham Kuyper was exactly right. Christ proclaims "mine" over everything: from parliaments to newspapers, from sports teams to factory floors, from internet browsing to completing tax returns—and from global church to a single household.

This passage is one of a little collection of New Testament passages (its parallels are Ephesians 5:21 – 6:9; 1 Timothy 5:1 – 6:2; Titus 2:1-10; 1 Peter 3:1-7) that have caused more sweat and ink-flow than most. To contemporary ears, these brief but punchy commands seem dated and even dangerous. This is why we need to see what Paul is, and, more significantly, is not saying. There are a few surprises in store.

### Christian home truths

In the Greek and Roman world, philosophers and ethical thinkers devoted a great deal of time and effort to considering what constituted "the good life". At one end of the spectrum, they might advise a young man setting out on adult life; they would suggest the kind of values and ambitions needed to leave a great legacy of public service or literary achievement. At the other, they advocated political systems that offered the greatest potential for civic health and security. Somewhere along the line, they would consider what would make for a good home in what are called "household codes".

A household back then was not what most of us in the West identify as such. Today, it might be made up of a couple, living temporarily with an average of 2.4 children. At some point, though, the children leave and the household reverts to just one generation. In the ancient world, as in many parts of today's world, three or even four generations would share a home, as well as various servants. And that pattern was not just for the rich. The Roman empire relied on slavery in the way that we depend on fossil fuels and transportation systems. Life without slaves was inconceivable.

Paul was clearly aware of these household codes in pagan philosophy, because he repeatedly uses the form. But he certainly did not share the pagan worldview. He radically adapted the form to make it profoundly Christian. There are major challenges in this passage for us and for our culture. But here I want to focus on the surprising positives we can glean for modern life.

## First surprise: respecting women, children and slaves

It is hard to imagine being a possession rather than a person. But under Roman law, if you were a woman or a slave, that is effectively what you were: a thing to be owned. Even free boys, despite clearly having the potential to grow into full manhood, still lived under the absolute authority of the head of the home. Any personal views or feelings that a "possession" might have were immaterial under the law and potentially ignored in the home (although family life being what it is, it is likely that most wives and children would not let most husbands get away with everything they wanted). The ultimate point, however, was one of responsibility. Just as a vacuum cleaner or laptop cannot be blamed for breaking (that can only be pinned on the designer, manufacturer or user), so a "possession" could not have responsibility for "its" actions.

It is total nonsense, of course, because people are not things. All remain created in God's image (regardless of their social or legal status), and so wives, children and slaves are bound to have opinions and responsibility—which is precisely Paul's point in these verses. That is why he insists on directly addressing each group in turn. In cities around the Roman world, women (**v 18**) and slaves (**v 22-24**), and their children (**v 20**), were being converted. God was at work among them. Not only that: God was using women and slaves, and no doubt also children, to further his kingdom. So just as Jesus did before him, Paul shows them the respect due to those with minds and wills of their own. This was revolutionary. No one had ever done that before. Every previous household code had been addressed deliberately and exclusively to the male head of the house.

Furthermore, he addresses each of these less powerful group *first*.

## Second surprise: the male challenge

Now consider what Paul actually says to the man of the house (**v 19, 21; 4:1**)—for in most households, the husband, father and slave-owner were one and the same. A pagan ethicist would give all kinds of helpful tips for how such a man could get the best out of the household team. That might include treating his subordinates well enough so that they would do what he wanted. But the emphasis was consistent: it helped *him* keep order among them.

There's not a bit of this with Paul. *Not once*—either here or in his other household codes—does Paul ever tell the men to make the women, children or slaves *do anything*. This is a fact overlooked by too many men who rule their homes like petty dictators, even justifying physical violence on the basis of these verses. They want to force everyone else to bend to their will. Instead, Paul gives some profoundly challenging and even subversive instructions to the men.

It is essential that all of Paul's commands are taken in pairs.

## Third Surprise: the Lord over all

Jesus is like a drumbeat through the whole section. Each household pairing is brought up short before God, and the instructions that Paul gives are all issued in the name of Christ:

■ Wives: "*as is fitting in the Lord*"

- Children: *"this pleases the Lord"*

- Slaves: *"for the Lord ... It is the Lord Christ you are serving"*

- Masters: *"you have a Master in heaven"*

How could any man finish reading this imagining that he is the lord of his little domestic empire? Christ alone holds ultimate authority over his home.

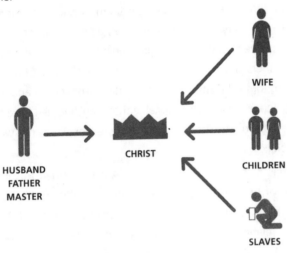

## Submission and service

The big problem comes with the "submission" word (**3:18**). Secular definitions are alarming: for example "accepting or yielding to a superior force or to the will of another person" (*Oxford English Dictionary*). That is the one thing many fear most.

Paul does not remind all believers here to "submit to one another out of reverence to Christ" (as he does in Ephesians 5:21). But there is no doubting the continued relevance of that truth. Submitting to another's authority ought never to be demeaning or diminishing—certainly not if that authority is wielded well. That is sadly quite a big "if". This is why a working biblical definition of submission should run more like this: "one equal person's voluntary acceptance of the authority of another equal person".

The problem today is that we tend to equate role with status and identity. For example, on meeting someone new, the second question we usually ask (after their name) is about their job. We will then be suitably impressed by a brain surgeon or an airline pilot, treating them slightly differently from someone who, say, delivers the mail or runs a supermarket checkout. But that is profoundly unchristian. Our roles should be irrelevant to our status in God's world. A person's job should make no difference to how we treat them. But it is no surprise that many find the very notion of submission demeaning; for the truth is that it has been used to justify demeaning and diminishing women, among others, for centuries. Men have not allowed Christ's grace-filled kingdom values to challenge worldly exploitation and abuse of women. Indeed, it is understandable that many women have thought that their terrible treatment (as mere possessions) was not worldly at all but biblical.

But this is so far from Paul's vision. A wife is called to submit not because of her husband, but "as is fitting in the Lord" (Colossians **3:18**). Christ has greater authority here than the husband. This is an essential relativising factor. In cases where there has been persistent abuse (physical, sexual or psychological for example), there will be times when that submission should stop. It should never be unthinking or blind obedience. At its heart is the respect and service due to Christ that is fundamental to being Christian.

When tied to the challenge for the husband, though, submission makes more sense. Decoupling **verse 18** from **verse 19** is a significant error; for submission is never to be advocated without the corresponding demand for husbands to "love your wives and … not be harsh with them". This love is not sentimental nor tokenism. This is sacrificial and demanding love. This is love like Christ's, which was expressed ultimately at the cross.

I remember one counselling situation, for example, where the husband, in a cold rage, railed against his wife for not submitting to him and called on me to insist that she did this. I flatly refused; because it was clear that the far greater priority was for him to love her so much that submitting to him would seem, and feel, like the most logical, wonderful and affirming thing she could do. If anything, then, the onus lies with the husband here, although each of us should be concerned first and foremost with what Jesus asks of us. Of

> We are all to bear with one another, forgive one another, and love one another.

course, every relationship is different, and crude generalisations are risky. It is another reason to be grateful that Paul was not a legalist—he does not give rules but shares wisdom.

These verses seem to be a summary of what Paul wrote elsewhere, and so it is important to hold them in combination with his very strong words to husbands in Ephesians 5:25-33. Of course, this is entirely consistent with what Paul urges for all Christians (Colossians 3:12-14). We are all to bear with one another, forgive one another, and love one another. All our relationships, but especially marriages, that get this right are windows into the gospel for us all.

Similar things need saying about children and parents, although the relationship is not identical to marriage. It is surprising that children are addressed at all—especially because the younger they are, the less responsibility they are deemed to have for their actions. But Paul honours them, as does the whole of Scripture. After all, the Lord Jesus frequently insisted that children be brought to him and even told their superior-feeling elders that they had much to learn from children (Mark 10:13-16). We might baulk at children being told to obey "parents in everything" because of the potential for abuse and harsh treatment. But this fits with the "whatever" of the previous section. Every aspect of our lives is to be submitted to Christ, and so for children, this means taking parents' authority seriously (Colossians **3:20**).

But as before, it cannot be dislocated from **verse 21**. It is shorthand, of course, so this is clearly not everything there is to say about parenting. But in so many of our homes, family life would be radically improved if we fathers took seriously Paul's command not to embitter or discourage our children. We have all failed at this; there is no doubt that we have not made it easy for our children to be obedient. Yet if we follow Christ, not infuriating our children with petty and pointless commands and boundaries is central to our discipleship. We all have so much to learn! One of the simplest but most helpful tips we personally were given as new parents was to be very quick to apologise to our children when we get things wrong. That has been vital!

## Wisdom and work

Among all the challenges associated with these verses, the presence of slavery even within a Christian household is the most perplexing factor here. No wonder the Bible seems outdated. Why doesn't Paul just abolish the whole thing?

One significant problem we have is that we in the West cannot divorce our view of slavery from the horrors of the transatlantic slave trade in the European colonies and southern United States. It is a horror which had cruel repercussions that have lasted to this day. The brutal inhumanity of that sinful system was exacerbated by the fact that it was bound to deep-rooted racism. It was unthinkable in the British Empire for a black man to have a white slave, for example. That was not the case in the Roman empire, where slavery was primarily the result of military conquest and economic suffering, but not due to race. There are documented instances of African Romans owning white slaves.

This is not to suggest that slavery was a positive thing, though. Far from it. But it was a fact of life in the ancient world. It perhaps helps to return to the analogy with fossil fuels. Our modern world is utterly dependent on them. Many of us would rather we ditched that dependence, but even the most radical of us realise this cannot happen overnight. It takes time to develop arguments to convince the sceptical, and find replacements to wean us off our addiction.

So it was with slavery. A society without slavery would have been unthinkable to people in the first century. But as we see here, and in a future chapter when we consider Philemon, Paul was determined to subvert it.

Imagine the surprise in the Colossian church as his letter was first read out. The slaves were perhaps mingling at the back, with the families of the well-to-do seated near the front. They were invisible and ignored. Worldly attitudes are hard to shake, after all. Then suddenly, Paul has something to say to the back rows. Of course, being told to be obedient to their masters was not exactly news. But to do so "with sincerity of heart and reverence for the Lord" (**v 22**)?

That was different.

Paul repeats his "whatever", and thereby begins his subversion. It doesn't matter what tasks slaves are assigned by their owners; Paul insists that they are serving a higher authority. They should do it with all their heart "as working for the Lord, not for human masters" (**v 23**). Not only that, but they had a reward to look forward to (**v 24**). That in itself was not their everyday experience—many would have felt lucky to have a day without being shouted at. But Jesus offers an eternal hope, which *includes* justice without favouritism (**v 25**). That is astonishing. Many Roman philosophers would have hated that. They assumed that because slaves were "human tools" (as Aristotle put it), how you treated your slaves had no ethical bearing. Paul rejects that outright. Slaves are human beings, pure and simple. Where they have suffered man's inhumanity to man—and each one has by the simple fact of being slaves—God will bring justice.

But Paul is at his most subversive when he addresses their owners. It must have been very uncomfortable

> Slaves are human beings, pure and simple. Where they have suffered man's inhumanity to man … God will bring justice.

for those (perhaps) sitting near the front of church to know that those at the back heard every word of this. Human masters were told to "provide your slaves with what is right and fair, because you know that you also have a Master in heaven" (**4:1**).

Of course, slavery is abhorrent and no one in their right mind could advocate it. Yet it is still a reality. At the time of writing, it is thought that over 40 million people globally live as slaves. Furthermore, what of those who are slaves in all but name? Countless millions have jobs for which they get paid, but it is often only a pittance, and they work in appalling circumstances with no job security or freedom. They often supply those of us in wealthy countries with the cheap products that enable us to spend our money on luxuries. Who can advocate for them but the free?

Slavery may seem remote for most of us, but the closest equivalent in our day is the world of employment. If we have a job, then we are either an employer or employee, and sometimes both at the same time. Exchange the words *slave* and *master* for these words, and then consider how different your workplace might be if everyone lived like this.

People might today talk about what goes on "behind closed curtains" being private. These days, with the advent of social media and the possibility of online surveillance, this is becoming less and less valid. But the fact remains that it has never actually been true. There is one who knows exactly what happens both behind closed curtains and deep within human hearts.

A number of my friends have this saying framed on their walls:

*"Christ is the head of this house, the unseen guest at every meal, the silent listener to every conversation."*

He knows it all. Nothing surprises him. Now, if it were not for God's grace, this would be deeply threatening and discomforting. For abusers of authority, this is an important corrective. But we can acknowledge our failure, knowing that God listens to us with grace. He motivates us to do and be something better than the evil desires of our hearts would lead us to. He lifts us out of our basest instincts into a life, and a home, that is truly different.

# Questions for reflection

1. The advice to husbands and wives in particular feels very countercultural, but, as we have seen, it was just as radical in the first century. How would you explain to an astonished outsider why this is such good news for men and women?

2. Paul speaks to slaves and masters (or employers and employees), and parents and children: Think about bad examples in each of these categories—in yourself or others. How might things be different if were living in obedience to Paul's wisdom here?

3. Identify one personal relationship you are struggling with at the moment. What command from these verses do you most need to hear and work through right now? How does the centrality of Jesus to all our relationships change everything?

# 9. PRAYER AND GOSPEL PARTNERSHIP

There is a famous sequence of images of President John F. Kennedy sitting at the Resolute desk in the Oval Office, taken in October 1963. There is nothing unusual in that. Every recent president has had countless photographs taken at that desk which was made from oak timbers from the British Arctic exploration ship *Resolute* and given by Queen Victoria in 1880. The photographs are made all the more poignant by the fact that Kennedy would be dead within a month, assassinated during a fateful trip to Dallas. But the most significant aspect of the photographs is that the president's young son, John Jr, has crawled into the footwell and is peering through the opened "secret" panel while his father works. The pictures became hugely popular, because John Jr had been the first child born to an elected US president in 80 years. They captured the essence of Kennedy's political appeal, a new and vigorous type of politician unlike any other twentieth-century leader before him.

But they also evoked the tragically short time that John Jr had with his father. His father's assassination took place just three days before his third birthday. The photographs capture a fleeting moment of loving intimacy and access that weeks later would be cruelly stolen from him. They point to an intimacy that is not just the privilege of presidential offspring. If we have come to know our heavenly Father through his Son, we have a greater confidence: access to the cosmic throne room, no less.

Paul is drawing his letter to a close. He has led his Colossian sisters and brothers on a breathtaking, cosmic voyage, covering everything from Christ's eternal identity and global mission down to the need for kindness in all our relationships and subversion of the culture of slavery. So what notes will he strike at the end?

After he has focused so consistently on Christ's lordship and our union with Christ, it is no accident that he ends with this focus on prayer. He opened the letter by revealing what he prayed for: thanksgiving for the Colossians' faith (1:3-8) and intercession for their growth (1:9-14). But his purpose now is far more significant than simply giving his letter a nice symmetry; for how else can we express and enjoy the privilege of being united to Jesus? We cannot see or touch him. We believe we "hear" him through his word, the Bible, but that doesn't mean we can describe the sound of his voice. It is all very indirect; we must take on trust the fact that it is him speaking to us through the Bible. But we can speak *to* him directly in prayer, trusting that he hears both our words and our groans (see Romans 8:26-27). We enjoy an extraordinary privilege.

# 1. Struggling in prayer

So Paul urges the Colossians, "Devote yourselves to prayer, being watchful and thankful" (Colossians **4:2**). It is a straightforward-enough statement. But if your prayer life is anything like mine, it is honoured more in the breach than the observance. That is because prayer is hard work. This should already be obvious from the letter. In 1:29, Paul wrote about how he strenuously contends with all the energy Christ so powerfully works in him. We saw then that he must be referring to his prayer for the Colossians, not least because of the parallel phrase to describe Epaphras's "wrestling in prayer" (**4:12**). This is the language of sweat and toil.

We will always give time to whatever we think is important. If we want to get into a football team, then we will make sacrifices to go to team practice. If we want to become an illusionist, we will spend hours practicing our sleight of hand to hide coins, playing cards and rabbits up our shirt cuffs. If we want to spend time with God, then we must decide to do so. None of these things will come effortlessly, and they will all entail forgoing other things we might enjoy.

But notice: yet again, Paul is not laying down the law here. He is not offering a list of rules and regulations by which we can measure our

> Take a cue from Jesus himself, who rose early in the morning to pray, when others were not around to disturb and distract him.

efforts; for prayerfulness can only be motivated by a response to God's grace. *That's* why we want to spend time with him! That is why Paul uses a word like "devote" (**v 2**). It suggests our sincere passion as much as our deliberate purpose. Sometimes there is a battle between our passion and our purpose, when we are distracted by other things that might be good in themselves to do, but that drag us away from our prayer times. This is probably why many take a cue from Jesus himself, who rose early in the morning to pray, when others were not around to disturb and distract him. But for some, evenings might be best, while others manage to use their daily commute.

What matters is that we each find a way to spend time in prayer, using whatever methods that genuinely help. There are no rules, but we can develop good disciplines. We are all different. I, for one, spent years feeling guilty for struggling to persist in prayer while sitting down in one place, as if this was the *only* way to be faithful as a Christian. It was quite the discovery to hear from a friend who said that he has his "quiet time" when out with the dog, and I can testify to finding that my best times of prayer have happened while doing the same thing. That is when using a smartphone app that keeps track of my prayer notes and prayer commitments can really come into its own. But it matters little what tools you use or what style you like. There are no rules. All that matters is that we devote ourselves to prayer!

## Be watchful

What does Paul have in mind when he urges his readers to "be watchful" (**v 2**)? There are some notable precedents for this word.

- Jesus called on his disciples to "keep watch" for his return because we do not know its timing (Matthew 25:13). Prayerfully waiting and crying out, "Come, Lord" (1 Corinthians 16:22) would certainly fit with what Paul wrote earlier (in Colossians 3:4).

- Jesus also told his disciples in Gethsemane to "watch and pray so that you will not fall into temptation" (Matthew 26:41). This would be wise advice in the light of Paul's grisly diagnosis of the human heart (Colossians 3:8-9).

We should certainly incorporate both senses of "being watchful" into our prayer lives. But there could be an even simpler interpretation—it is simply a matter of being watchful for answers to the prayers we pray. That is why keeping a prayer diary can be so helpful. We can look back and realise how many answers to prayer we have forgotten.

## Be thankful

It is almost as if Paul cannot give an instruction without slipping in thankfulness as an afterthought. Except it is no such thing. Grace and gratitude clearly have the same roots in English and so do the words they translate in Paul's original Greek. But that should be no surprise. How can a recipient of divine grace not be profoundly grateful?

So this makes for a useful diagnostic tool for the spiritual health of disciples. Just ask how thankful they are.

## 2. Praying for preaching

In chapter 1, Paul proved his partnership with the Colossians by sharing what he prayed for them. Now in **4:3-4** he asks them to reciprocate. Will they join with him by praying for his ministry and mission? Having touched on the fact, back in Colossians 1, that prayer requests reveal a great deal about a person's priorities, we are in for quite a surprise now.

Imagine that some bad news comes in of a leader who has had a significant impact on your church—perhaps as the original planter, or the one who **ordained** or commissioned your leaders. He is in jail! After the initial panic and confusion, various inescapable questions linger. Surely there's been a huge mistake? Surely he doesn't deserve it? What's going to happen to us? Are we next? But some might voice niggling doubts. How do we know there's no smoke without fire? Perhaps he really did do something terrible. And so the questions continue.

We know from the rest of the New Testament that Paul's suffering was the direct consequence of his politically-incorrect ministry. Proclaiming Christ the Lord unavoidably put him in conflict with Caesar the Lord. That is why Paul was "in chains" (**v 3**). But isn't it astonishing that he has said nothing about it until the very end of the letter? Then, when he does mention it in the course of his prayer requests, what does he ask for?

We would naturally expect him to ask to get out of jail. After all, he was there unjustly. But that is not quite what he says. It is more ambiguous: "that God may open a door for our message, so that we may proclaim the mystery of Christ". This might express the desire for his cell door to spring open. That had happened to Peter (Acts 12:5-10). It had even happened to Paul and Silas in Philippi (Acts 16:25-28). But whether or not Paul stays behind bars seems to be less of a priority than the opportunity he has to proclaim Christ. That is far more important. If he has to do that from within prison (in order to reach the imperial palace guard, as he writes in Philippians

1:13), then so be it. What Paul realises more than anything, though, is that his words alone are ineffectual and feeble without the empowering work of God. Only God can bring the message to life in such a way as to raise the spiritually dead to life. That is why praying for evangelism is so urgent and vital.

But it is not simply the moment of proclamation that concerns Paul. He wants them to pray he would do it "clearly, as I should" (Colossians **4:4**). Elsewhere (Ephesians 6:19-20) Paul requests prayer that he would be fearless; here he asks for clarity. It is not simply a matter of clear delivery (although that is certainly important). It is more that the content of his message is sufficiently clear (and without any cross-cultural pitfalls that can be such a distraction) for his hearers to understand it fully. That takes preparation. In fact, as a general rule from my experience of training preachers, the less preparation a preacher does, the less clear and coherent their message will be. In our prayers for the preachers in our church, we should frequently include this crucial element of their preparation.

But there is a further element to this that we should not overlook. Paul reminds us that his message is "the mystery of Christ" (Colossians **4:3**). This throws us back to 1:27 and 2:1-4, where we see that what God had kept secret for generations was now on public display: the truths that Christ is himself God's treasury for wisdom *and* that he can live within Gentiles as well as Jews. In proclaiming this clearly, Paul wants to be sure that no part of this revelation is kept back—*all* must know it *all*.

## 3. Preaching with grace

Yet again, Paul cannot resist slipping from thoughts of his own ministry to considering that of the Colossians. Yet again, the key thought is grace: for if the message is one of grace, then the way it is communicated must be characterised by graciousness.

Marshall McLuhan was a brilliant Canadian thinker and teacher in the middle of the twentieth century, known for identifying the development of "the global village" and predicting the internet thirty years before it became reality. He would make deliberately provocative statements to force people to think, but his ideas have been immensely influential. In particular, he coined the phrase "The medium is the message", and tried very hard to help people grasp the effect that new media are having on us. So he famously said:

> "The content or message of any particular medium has about as much importance as the stenciling on the casing of an atomic bomb." (*Essential McLuhan*, page 238)

So you might decide to stencil the words "Give Peace A Chance" or even "Jesus Loves You" onto the side of a missile with the best of intentions, but the medium (in this case, a nuclear warhead) will totally eclipse your message.

It is an extreme example, to be sure. But it goes a little way to explain why our presentation of a message that is so full of wonder and joy can fail to hit its mark. It is because the Christians proclaiming it show so little generosity of spirit and tone as they do so. We cannot excuse ourselves by saying, "But my message is full of grace".

So as we seek to present Christ to this generation, this must be part of being "wise in the way you act towards outsiders" (**v 5**). That must in part mean being sensitive to the circumstances and concerns of those we are seeking to reach. Of course, many of us (myself included) find it much easier to do this than to "make the most of every opportunity". We can use our sensitivity as an excuse to overlook the opportunities that come our way. But Paul's concern seems in these verses to be to temper Christians with a more hot-headed and abrasive evangelism style.

There is a word in **verse 6** that often gets missed: "conversation". Paul does not envisage every believer preaching in the streets. But he does expect people to talk with family, friends and neighbours. As a result of everyday interactions, he longs for all to feel as comfortable with talking about Jesus as they might be about their jobs or the sports results. Conversation implies dialogue and mutual interest, which hopefully means saying things that prompt questions. "Seasoned with salt" seems to have been an old Jewish idiom for keeping things interesting. That can be through being quirky, or provocative, or surprising. The key is to avoid being predictable or banal, because we long for conversation to lead to a new recognition that Christ is indeed Lord.

So we must take the questions people ask us seriously. In fact, if it is genuine, there is no such thing as a question that is too stupid or too hostile. We need to be ready for anything, which is presumably what lies behind Paul's desire for the believers to "know how to answer everyone". We cannot always help it if a question catches us out the first time. But it is irresponsible to be caught out by the same question a second time. We need to do our preparation as well.

Above all, our medium—in this case, conversation—must "be always full of grace", because our message of the mystery of Christ is entirely about grace.

## Questions for reflection

1. What do you think "watchful" means (v 2)? What might this look like in practice in your prayer life?

2. Despite the costs involved, why can we be confident when we share the gospel with others?

3. Do you have the kind of friendships and relationships that mean you are able to have conversations about the gospel? How will you "make the most of every opportunity"?

## PART TWO

This will sound entirely obvious. But it needs stating, nevertheless:

- Christianity is not primarily a set of **doctrinal** statements, important though they are. After all, God did not reveal himself in a volume of **systematic theology**.

- Christianity is not primarily a culture, although there is no doubting its astonishing, world-changing legacy in realms as diverse as politics and economics, philanthropy and charity, art and music, literature and philosophy, architecture and society. God's handiwork is evident in all these spheres and more.

- Christianity is not even primarily a story, although it is without question the greatest story ever told (despite perhaps not necessarily being the best understood). After all, it is unlikely we will need our Bibles in eternity when we are in Christ's presence.

Christianity is about God's kingdom. It is Christ and his People. It's about the people!

The Scriptures are full of individuals. Some we learn a great deal about; some only get a fleeting walk-on part. But they all seem remote because we have yet to meet any of them personally. We will, of course, but not yet. To learn what they are like, we must take others' words for it. But we should never race through the Bible's lists of names, including those that feature in Paul's letters. Each one has a significance in the kingdom. Each name has something to teach us about the kingdom. Each one is part of the whole point of the gospel.

So even though we don't know these individuals, they are part of us and we are part of them if we all share our union in Christ. This is what the kingdom is all about.

## Despatched from the prison cell

Having mentioned his imprisonment only in passing in the previous passage, Paul shows that is not unaware of the Colossians' concerns.

Paul has a purpose in how he describes Tychicus and Onesimus. These are not simply warm pleasantries.

He knows they will want news of their apostle. But instead of filling up valuable parchment with details that do not especially serve his spiritual purpose in writing, he knows that all the gaps will be filled in by this letter's couriers: Tychicus and Onesimus. "They will tell you everything that is happening here" (**v 9**).

They were clearly well known to the Colossians. But Paul has a purpose in how he describes them. These are not simply warm pleasantries.

## Tychicus: the gospel partner

Paul praises the significance of Tychicus to his work to pave the way for Tychicus to have a spiritual role in the Colossian church, calling him "a dear brother, a faithful minister and fellow servant in the Lord" (**v 7**). These are wonderful accolades and they show how valued a team-player Tychicus was. Paul did not have a specific church post in mind when he referred to him as "minister" (the word did not carry that connotation at this early stage). Instead, it pointed to his character rather than a job description, for his service of others was motivated by faithfulness to the Lord. So to be a minister and a servant in the Lord effectively meant the same thing, with the added aspect that Tychicus was Paul's "fellow". They were in this business together.

This meant that while Paul was stuck in prison, the Colossians would not miss out—Tychicus would bring them up to date ("that you may know about our circumstances" (**v 8**), and he would explain anything from the letter they were unclear about ("that he may encourage your hearts"). In a small reflection of our Lord's concern for his mother while hanging on the cross, Paul is looking to serve and love these as-yet unmet sisters and brothers, albeit by sending others to them.

## Onesimus: the beloved brother

Now, **verse 9** raises a trickier issue: the slave called "Useful" (the meaning of the name Onesimus). We will explore this in more depth in the next chapter when we come to Paul's letter to Philemon, which was almost certainly being carried by Tychicus in the same package as the letter to the Colossians. The Colossian Christians would have known Onesimus. That was not in doubt; he "is one of you". The problem was the kind of reception he would receive when he got to Colossae. As we will see, he had fled Colossae in dubious circumstances: he was a runaway slave. Under Roman law, this was punishable by death. But Paul sends him home.

So what does that mean? Does Paul approve of his enslavement? What does he expect Onesimus' owner, Philemon, to do? How should the church respond? We will come to these questions later. But for now, notice how Paul describes Onesimus: as "our faithful and dear brother" (**v 9**). These are precisely the same accolades he gave Tychicus in **verse 7**. Paul implies there is no distinction of status between them whatsoever. But the implications of this go further. Would Philemon think the same? After all, as Paul has said earlier in the letter:

"Here there is no Gentile or Jew, circumcised or uncircumcised, barbarian, Scythian, slave or free, but Christ is all, and is in all."

(3:11)

Paul clearly hopes that Philemon will think as he does.

## Greetings from the Ephesus gospel team

There is some debate about the dating of Paul's imprisonment as he wrote this letter. One suggestion is that he wrote Colossians when in Rome, which is when he wrote one of the other "prison letters": Philippians. However, it does make sense to see Colossians as written earlier, from Ephesus (hinted at in 2 Corinthians 1:8). As Ephesus was a major city in the region, communication with the cities of the Lycus Valley was frequent and relatively straightforward. They were only around 200 km (125 miles) apart, and so it is entirely plausible that Epaphras and Onesimus met Paul there—rather than in Rome, which was well over 2500 km (1000 miles) away.

As Paul seeks to deepen the connections with the Colossians, he makes the most of the number of friends they have in common.

## Three Jews

Despite being a former Pharisee who had persecuted the church, Paul had a profound commitment to introducing his fellow Jews to their Messiah; which is why it must have been so heartbreaking to mention that Aristarchus, Mark and Jesus Justus were "the only Jews among my fellow workers for the kingdom of God" (Colossians **4:10-11**). It is no surprise therefore that he found "they have proved a comfort to me". Paul was nothing like the toughened and heartless lone ranger that he is sometimes portrayed to be. If one thing is clear on every page of his writings, it is that serving Christ was costly for him. There was nothing he would rather do, but it profoundly affected him, physically, psychologically and spiritually. He needed his friends. He could never have done what he did alone. **Verse 11** is the only place where we hear of Jesus Justus, but the other two men feature elsewhere in the New Testament:

> Paul was nothing like the toughened and heartless lone ranger that he is sometimes portrayed to be.

- ■ Aristarchus (**v 10**) was not just a colleague but Paul's "fellow-prisoner". We know little about him, except that he originated from Macedonia and got swept up in the mob violence in Ephesus with Paul (Acts 27:2; 19:29-30). This verse is the only place where we learn that he is Jewish.

- ■ Paul and (John) Mark had had a rocky relationship after badly falling out in the past (see Acts 13:3; then 15:36-41), when Paul and Barnabas parted company over whether or not to keep Mark in the team. Yet they have clearly been reconciled by this point—and perhaps Paul has been reconciled with Barnabas as well. Presumably, a visit by Mark to Colossae is on the cards. Paul wants to ensure that past disagreements do not provoke a less-than-positive welcome.

## Three Gentiles

Some in the Colossian church may perhaps have hoped for Epaphras to come home as the letter's courier. After all, he, like Onesimus, was "one of you" (Colossians **4:12**) and similarly servant-hearted. But Paul wants to reassure them that his absence does not betray a waning commitment to them. Far from it. We learn in Philemon v 23 that he is Paul's "fellow prisoner in Christ", and, as we have seen, he is "always wrestling in prayer for you, that you may stand firm in all the will of God, mature and fully assured" (Colossians **4:12**). Geographical separation in no sense means spiritual separation.

But it is clear that Epaphras has commitments that go beyond Colossae. He has a vision for the whole of the Lycus Valley (hence the mention of Laodicea and Hierapolis in **verse 13**) and perhaps even further (which would explain his presence with Paul in Ephesus). One of the great sadnesses of ministry is the impact that moving on has on our relationships. It is an inescapable consequence of investing deeply in the lives of others. Yet, as someone once quipped, Christians never need say "goodbye", but only "*au revoir*" (French for "until the next time"). Because we are united to Christ, we are bound to one another—for eternity.

Luke and Demas also send greetings (**v 14**). Both feature elsewhere, although later Demas sadly abandons the cause (2 Timothy 4:10). Even though Paul does not say so, it is quite possible that both men had been slaves. Both are, by inference, Gentiles. (Paul's Greek in Colossians **4:11** is quite tricky to translate, but the NIV makes a good judgment in seeing the Jews restricted to the group of three in

**verses 10-11**. This is why Epaphras, Luke and Demas are presumed, therefore, to be Gentile.)

The names Luke and Demas are shortened forms (often given to slaves by their owners). But even more significantly, we learn that Luke was a doctor, and the vast majority of first-century doctors were slaves. (See Michael Card, *A Better Freedom*, page 102.) The wealthy or aristocratic would never want to get involved in anything as squalid, and the poor would never be able to afford the training. Owners would see the chance of making money out of intelligent slaves, and so invest in having them trained as doctors. It would certainly explain Luke's preoccupation in his Gospel for society's outsiders and the marginalised.

This is speculative of course, but not unreasonable. It would certainly give added poignancy to this letter's key theme: namely, Christ destroying the social divisions of class and slave status. Paul was sending Onesimus back with this letter, but he did not bat an eyelid about having former slaves on his team. They were as valued members as anyone else. To Luke, for one thing, we owe a great debt for writing an "orderly account" of what Jesus began to do (in his Gospel) and continued to do (in the book of Acts). It is intriguing therefore that in Mark and Luke, Paul travelled with two of the New Testament's Gospel-writers. In contrast to what sceptics suggest, Paul's message is entirely consistent with what Jesus himself preached, and with all four Gospel accounts. We cannot and should not drive a wedge between Paul and the rest of the New Testament.

Paul clearly practised what he preached. These Gentile names reflect his understanding of the lordship of Christ over a new community. He lived out the reconciliation he proclaimed. It raises questions for our own communities and churches. Do they reflect the same willingness not just to be reconciled, but to develop, train and work with those who are different from us? It is quite something to consider that some of Paul's most trusted companions (see how often Luke accompanied him, in the book of Acts) were the most marginalised socially. Could the same be said of us?

## Greetings to the Lycus valley gospel partnership

The closing greetings (unusually) pick out the few individuals in the Lycus Valley that Paul does know (**v 15**). As we have seen, Laodicea was just up the road from Ephesus. In common with nearly all the churches of the first century, the believers met in homes, which is why Paul acknowledges "Nympha and the church in her house". We have no idea what Archippus' issue was, although it does seem a little harsh to pick up on it so publicly! Whatever his ministry was, persevering to completion is always a good idea, though (**v 17**)!

It is no surprise that a letter so concerned with universal truths was to be shared beyond its initial recipients. Timothy and Titus evidently thought that Paul's letters to them were too important to keep to themselves, which is how they ended up in the New Testament. But here we find that Paul intended this one (at least) to be sent up the road (**v 16**). We cannot be sure what Paul meant by the Laodicean letter, though a convincing case has been made for it being what we know as Ephesians. They cover very similar ground and seem to have been written at the same time. If that is the case, what a privilege it is to have an apostolic window into the life of God's church in this tiny ancient corner of the world.

At this point, Paul takes up the quill and signs off in his own hand (**v 18**). He has been dictating the whole thing so far, which was his common practice (see also 1 Corinthians 16:21; 2 Thessalonians 3:17 and, of course, Philemon v 19). But just as professionals might "top and tail" a letter typed up by an assistant with a greeting and a signature, so Paul does here. His parting shots are very revealing.

## Remember my chains

The gospel is so clearly Paul's priority over everything, even his own personal comfort and security. But this hardly means he would not prefer freedom. The request in Colossians **4:18** to "remember" is presumably a plea for prayer and solidarity—for how easy it would be for the Colossians to allow shame at his imprisonment to create a reticence to identify as Paul's brothers and sisters.

## Grace be with you

Paul's final statement might sound like a standard, and even hollow, farewell. But after all we have learned in Colossians, it is far from that. For we have travelled far in the realms of Christ Jesus, the Lord of all. But he is no dictator Caesar, who simply demands that his followers die for him to sustain his reign. As we saw in the introduction, Caesar claimed to offer forgiveness, peace, and provision, and in a limited sense he was able to do that. But Christ actually delivers it—for all eternity. He is God's King, who was crowned on a cross. His victorious death brings complete forgiveness for every sin, ushers in eternal peace with our Creator, and lavishes upon us the treasures of his heaven. Having reconciled us to our Father, he reconciles us with one another. He truly showers us with his grace.

God's grace can only provoke our gratitude to God. And our gratitude must surely work out in graciousness to one and all, whether to those who are part of the body, or towards outsiders who ply us with questions.

Grace. Gratitude. Graciousness. This is lordship the like of which the world has never seen. What an extraordinary privilege to know it first hand. So as Christ has shared his grace with us, we, with Paul, share grace with all.

## Questions for reflection

1. Although the theological themes of this letter are cosmic, the application is always personal and relational. How connected are you to the struggles and lives of real people? Or is your Christianity more a matter of head knowledge and theology only?

2. Paul's descriptions of his friends focus on their hard work and service for the gospel. How can we encourage one another to persevere in our service of the Lord, his people, and those who do not yet know him?

3. How does the prayer of Epaphras (v 12) sum up the big message of Colossians? How would you summarise this letter's message? Write a single sentence that captures its themes.

# 10. THE CHAINED PRISONER AND THE RUNAWAY SLAVE

Gold is valuable for several reasons. Its rarity is an obvious factor. Its glistening beauty, especially in certain kinds of light, is another, making it ideal for jewellery and decoration. Being so soft and malleable is a significant help for that. But it also has unusual chemical properties. As one of the few "noble metals", it resists corrosion or reaction with other chemicals.

These properties make it relatively simple to prove its presence, which was crucial for gold traders before modern scientific resources. So they would administer an "acid test". The specimen to be scrutinised would be rubbed against a dark stone to leave a visible trace. The tester would pour some *aqua fortis* (nitric acid) onto the stone. If the trace was not gold, it would immediately dissolve. If it remained, *aqua regia* (*aqua fortis* combined with hydrochloric acid) would be used. This is much stronger and is one of the very few substances that does dissolve gold. If the trace then disappeared, there could be confidence that the original object was indeed made of gold.

We can see this unique letter to Philemon as an acid test for the truths Paul taught in its companion letter to the Colossians. Some have thought its inclusion in the New Testament a mistake because it seems, at first sight, so incongruous and slight. After all, despite the other individuals and churches named in the letter, it is essentially private correspondence:

> "Paul, a prisoner of Christ Jesus, and Timothy our brother, to Philemon our dear friend and fellow worker—also to Apphia our sister and Archippus our fellow soldier—and to the church that meets in your home." (Philemon **v 1-2**)

The fact that Timothy (**v 1**) is not described as a fellow prisoner either here or in Colossians 1:1 (unlike Aristarchus in Colossians 4:10) suggests that he is with Paul in Ephesus but not under arrest. His inclusion here may well be a formality, but the other names are not: Apphia (Philemon **v 2**) is most probably Philemon's wife, and Archippus (mentioned in Colossians 4:17 because of that mysterious unfinished ministry) is a senior believer in Colossae. For this letter concerns an issue that can never be a private matter, even if Philemon might have wished it could. Paul knows that it will affect the church as a whole, and not just the fellowship meeting in Philemon's home—for it will function as an acid test for the very message Paul preaches. It is one thing to believe that Christ reconciles us to God and to one another; it is another thing to see that lived out in a small community in which everyone knows everyone. That is why Philemon **v 3** is no formality either. Peace and grace are very precisely what this letter is about: God's peace and grace and the resulting peace and grace displayed in his people.

> It is one thing to believe that Christ reconciles us to God and to one another; it is another thing to see that lived out in a small community in which everyone knows everyone.

In writing this letter, therefore, Paul is rubbing Philemon's discipleship against a dark stone. How Philemon responds will reveal whether or not it is composed of true gold.

# 1. Evidence of true discipleship

There is no doubting Philemon's conversion, nor the fact that he was a much-loved figure in the Christian community in the Lycus valley. He was evidently one of the few Colossian Christians that Paul knew personally, and the apostle's prayers are filled with happy and positive memories. It seems that Philemon was an easy person to be thankful for:

"I hear about your love for all his holy people and your faith in the Lord Jesus." (v 4-5)

He was a model of the very thing for which the Colossian church was known: love without discrimination or favouritism (Colossians 1:4).

Furthermore, Paul says, "Your love has given me great joy and encouragement, because you, brother, have refreshed the hearts of the Lord's people" (Philemon v 7). Paul's phrase at the end of that verse is hard to translate: "refreshing hearts" sounds a little limp. The verb he uses here had military origins, describing the recuperation an army might need after being exhausted by a forced march. Philemon was like that: precisely the type of person every church needs in tough times. Perhaps he was the Colossians' equivalent of Barnabas, the "son of encouragement" (Acts 4:36).

So here is a man who could, to paraphrase the apostle James, show his faith by his deeds (see James 2:18). But that faith was about to face its biggest trial yet. It might not have seemed big in the grand scheme of things, but it will have significant implications. It would prove whether or not the community of grace that Paul calls us to aspire to in Colossians is realistic and workable.

So notice what he prays for. As so often, the content of Paul's prayer reveals the major themes of this letter that it introduces.

"I pray that your partnership with us in the faith may be effective in deepening your understanding of every good thing we share for the sake of Christ." (Philemon v 6)

## Partnership

The word translated by "partnership" (*koinōnia*) is hard to capture precisely. It has often been conveyed as "fellowship" but that seems too passive; an alternative is "sharing" but that also feels a bit too weak. The essence is a deep and mutual bond: a belonging to one another that leads to serving with one another. It is actually an outflowing of our common bond with Christ. It is joyful and active, committed and sustained. And Philemon was already on the team. He was a committed gospel partner with Paul.

But the Christian life is never static. It can never be a question of putting our feet up after attaining certain levels of discipleship. We press on towards the goal for which God has called us heavenwards, as Paul wrote elsewhere (Philippians 3:14).

So, Paul prays.

## Deepening understanding

Discipleship cannot be mindless, nor can it be simply instinctive. It demands careful thought, especially as we enter new circumstances or different stages of life. The behaviour patterns in a previous situation may not help us now. For example, how we live out our faith as university students will not necessarily prepare us for life in the office or factory in which we have far less autonomy. We may face ethical dilemmas in the world of work that had never even occurred to us beforehand. So we must think. We cannot and should not do that alone—we have our Bibles to shape us, our pastors to teach us and our church to uphold us. This is not about being intellectual but faithful. It is thus a direct application of Paul's clothing image in Colossians:

> "you have taken off your old self with its practices and have put on the new self, which is being renewed in knowledge in the image of its Creator." (Colossians 3:9-10)

New clothes demand renewed knowledge. Only then can we share "every good thing" (Philemon **v 6**).

## Every good thing

You will never find in Scripture an exhaustive list of good things to do. That would be a book filled with law not grace. The Bible is not designed to give us rules for every eventuality, but to equip us with wisdom to...

> "live a life worthy of the Lord and please him in every way: bearing fruit in every good work, growing in the knowledge of God."
> (Colossians 1:10; see also Ephesians 2:10; 2 Timothy 3:17)

However, there is no doubting that Paul has a very particular fruit that he is praying for Philemon to display. The letter to the Colossians provided the framework; this letter adds the specifics.

## 2. Evidence of true usefulness

Paul knows all too well he can pull rank. He is an apostle!

> "...in Christ I could be bold and order you to do what you ought to do yet I prefer to appeal to you on the basis of love."
> (Philemon **v 8-9**)

Love is key because, as Paul has already said, that is how Philemon's faith in Christ is proved genuine: he loves Christ's people. Of course, love *is* a command in Scripture—which proves that it cannot simply be a sentiment or fiery passion. After all, if Christ's love for us had depended on him feeling loving, he would never have gone to the cross. In Gethsemane, he was filled with the darkest emotions of terror and despair, which is why he needed to decide to go to the cross (see Luke 22:39-44). He had to *decide* to love.

But Paul doesn't want Philemon to love just because Paul has told him to but because the gospel makes it the right thing to do. He wants Philemon to *want* to love. So now at last, after Paul has laid the groundwork, we get to the nitty-gritty. It perhaps feels a little like emotional arm-twisting here, but identity is crucial to Paul's entire appeal. Notice how Paul describes each person involved in the conversation:

| Paul | Philemon | Onesimus |
|------|----------|----------|
| • A prisoner of Christ Jesus (v 1) <br> • An old man and a prisoner of Christ Jesus (v 9) <br> • Philemon's partner (v 17) | • Dear friend and fellow worker (v 1) <br> • Brother (v 7) | • My son. Became my son while I was in chains (v 10) <br> • Was useless, now useful (v 11) <br> • My very heart (v 12) <br> • Better than a slave, a dear brother to Philemon, fellow man and brother in the Lord (v 16) |

"It is as none other than Paul—an old man and now also a prisoner of Christ Jesus— that I appeal to you for my son Onesimus, who became my son while I was in chains. Formerly he was useless to you, but now he has become useful both to you and to me." (Philemon **v 9-11**)

It is only now that Paul mentions Onesimus by name. Philemon would undoubtedly have seen him already, since Onesimus accompanied Tychicus, the courier of the letters (Colossians 4:7-9). That would have been a surprise in itself. But Philemon probably had no inkling at all of what Paul expected to happen next.

Reading any New Testament letter is a little like sitting on a bus and overhearing another passenger talking to a friend on the phone. We can usually make an educated guess as to what the friend is saying, since most of the time people are rarely that creative when explaining where they are ("I'm on the bus"), what they are doing ("I'm going to be a bit late") and how they feel ("I'm really hungry")! One memorable exception occurred when I was waiting at the gate in an American airport, and a surgeon who had missed an earlier flight was calling ahead with (very loud) instructions to prepare for an operation later that day. I understood very little about the operation, but his graphic descriptions still left me feeling nauseous.

So what can we figure out here?

■ Philemon is a key member of the Colossian church who had been converted through Paul (Philemon **v 19**). He owns a slave by the name of Onesimus—a name which ironically enough means "useful".

■ Onesimus has absconded from his owner, quite possibly stealing funds from Philemon (how else would he survive?). In parts of the Roman Empire, the maximum punishment for this was death, although it is not possible to be sure whether or not this was followed in the Turkish provinces. So an owner who spared his runaway slave the death penalty would have been very gracious indeed (by the standards of the day).

■ Onesimus finds his way to Paul—which is one reason for suspecting Paul's imprisonment happened in Ephesus (since it is much closer than Rome). Is this because Onesimus heard Paul mentioned in the church that meets in Philemon's home in Colossae? Or because he searched out Epaphras, whom he'd known from before? Whatever the reason, Paul leads Onesimus to Christ (**v 10**). This new spiritual reality has transformed him. Formerly "Useless Useful" is now truly useful (**v 11**).

The term "butterfly effect" comes from the study of weather systems, whereby small causes can have larger effects. It was coined by Edward Lorenz, who was analysing the origins of tornadoes, and suggested that the accumulative effect of minute events (even as tiny as the flapping of a butterfly's wing) can have vast and devastating consequences several weeks later. When weather systems are modelled on a computer, entirely different outcomes result from changing the slightest initial details. It is a powerful image to describe the sheer complexity of our world.

The butterfly effect of that Colossian slave's step of faith would have truly historic and global consequences. In terms of God's kingdom, he was no human tool. He was now Paul's son and our brother. Paul could never have imagined the precise details of the consequences of Onesimus' conversion, but he clearly recognised its significance.

This was a test case of his most cherished beliefs about the kingdom of God.

We will come back to how Paul develops his argument in the letter. But for now, we can learn much from how Paul sees this new convert. Onesimus has aligned his affections and perspective to those of Christ himself.

> The butterfly effect of that slave's step of faith would have truly historic and global consequences.

The English evangelical leader John Stott had been a lifelong bachelor when he died in 2011 aged ninety. In common with many of his generation, he rarely spoke openly about private matters, which is what made the occasions when he did all the more significant. In an interview for Al Hsu's book about singleness, he spoke honestly about occasionally feeling lonely and envying families. But clearly that was not the norm, because he then said this:

> "In addition, single people are wise to develop as many friendships as possible, with people of all ages and both sexes. For example, although I have no children of my own, I have hundreds of adopted nephews and nieces all over the world, who call me 'Uncle John.' I cherish these affectionate relationships; they greatly lessen, even if they do not altogether deaden, occasional pangs of loneliness." (*The Single Issue*, page 202)

Stott was taking a leaf from the apostle Paul's book, for he clearly had sons and daughters wherever he travelled. They really were family now. This is yet another reminder that serving God's kingdom should never be about building empires (as if congregations and church networks *belong* to any individual leaders) but should always be about growing families. It is about relationships. It is *people*. Paul has described others as sons or children before:

- The Corinthian believers (1 Corinthians 4:14; 2 Corinthians 6:13)

- The Galatian believers (Galatians 4:19)

- Timothy (1 Corinthians 4:17; Philippians 2:22; 1 Timothy 1:2; 2 Timothy 2:1)

- Titus (Titus 1:4)

Like any good parent, Paul seeks the flourishing of his children. He wants them to grow up and thrive, to make the most of the lives God has given them. That is why he serves them with everything he has.

Very few of us will ever have the opportunities that Paul, and indeed John Stott, had to influence individual lives in many different countries. But that is beside the point. All of us have family ties to those in our local church fellowships—we are all each others' brothers and sisters. And just as Paul encouraged the Colossians to teach one another the message of Christ, so we are to invest in each others lives. The more we do that, the more we will find ourselves committed to each others' welfare. We may even find ourselves to be not just spiritual siblings but spiritual parents in Christ.

## Questions for reflection

1. When a complex and difficult question or life choice faces you, where do you look to inform your choice? What principles does the letter of Philemon suggest for these moments?

2. Read again the encouraging description of Philemon in Philemon v 4-7. How do you think you match up to these qualities? What might Paul have written about you?

3. What tensions are there for a Christian who knows that their true family is those with whom they are united in Christ?

## PART TWO

### Master and slave indebted to Paul

The 18th-century movement to abolish slavery is one of the brightest moments in human history. In the British context, William Wilberforce is justly famous, but what of Thomas Clarkson, John Newton, Thomas Fowell Buxton, Hannah More, Olaudah Equiano or Mary Prince? Arguably, each deserves to be far better known.

They were not the only campaigners, by any stretch, but these great ones were united in their hatred of slavery by a greater love. All were compelled by their love for Jesus Christ. One of their most powerful campaign tools was a medallion produced in huge quantities by the renowned potter and industrialist, Josiah Wedgwood. This depicted in profile a kneeling but chained African slave, looking up and pleading. Around the rim ran these words: "Am I not a man and a brother?" The image managed the eighteenth-century equivalent of going viral, and without doubt helped to garner mass support for the anti-slavery movement.

There is no doubt that this branding and strapline was influenced by Paul's letter, in particular Philemon **verse 16**, which is why **verse 12** comes as such a shock to us: "I am sending him—who is my very heart—back to you". To which we cry, "Why?" How could Paul do this, especially now that Onesimus had come to Christ? How could that possibly make any sense?

### 1. Paul's reasons and God's purpose

We need to ask what options Paul had available to him. Just as we cannot decide on a whim to rid the world of fossil fuels, however much we might long to—after all, even environmental activists still find themselves travelling by trains, planes and automobiles—so Paul couldn't abolish slavery. He never set out to do that. But he could subvert it. This is exactly what we see him doing, as gently and subtly as he can within the context of a delicate pastoral conundrum; for he was committed to Philemon's discipleship as much as he was to that of Onesimus. He would not go in with all guns blazing.

The first thing he does here is to reassure Philemon that "useless Onesimus" really is useful now: "I would have liked to keep him with me so that he could take your place in helping me while I am in chains for the gospel" (**v 13**). Paul's

> Paul couldn't abolish slavery. He never set out to do that. But he could subvert it.

subtlety here is shown by his confidence in Philemon's friendship, knowing that he would love to have given support from outside prison walls. Who knows? If Onesimus had not absconded, Philemon may perhaps have sent him in his place anyway. So Paul is suggesting that things actually worked out quite well!

Of course, he would love to hold on to Onesimus. But he also wants to preserve his valued friendship with Philemon, not to mention the vexed legal issue of harbouring a runaway slave (as if he, the prisoner in Ephesus, wasn't in trouble enough). There is a tightrope to walk here, beset with all kinds of moral dilemmas. Paul is sure about what ought to happen. But he wants Philemon to be sure too, so that he actually desires the same thing (**v 14**). Sending Onesimus back is in part proof of his respect for Philemon's maturity and responsibility.

Paul's most daring reason, though, makes perfect sense if you believe in God's sovereignty and providence. There's no doubt that Paul believes it, but he realises that it may be too soon for Philemon to apply that to this situation. He may still feel too angry and betrayed to see any good in Onesimus's flight. That is why Paul introduces the reason with "perhaps" (**v 15**). This demonstrates real pastoral tact, and many of us could learn to better emulate Paul instead of blurting out doctrines of which only we ourselves are fully convinced. But this gets to the heart of Paul's argument.

"Perhaps the reason he was separated from you for a little while was that you might have him back for ever—no longer as a slave, but better than a slave, as a dear brother. He is very dear to me but even dearer to you, both as a fellow man and as a brother in the Lord." (**v 15-16**)

So what could God be up to? The Bible is full of precedents for God bringing good out of human disobedience. The most relevant actually comes from another story of slavery: **Joseph's** sale into slavery by his brothers. Years later, having become Egyptian Prime Minister, he could look back on it all in the confidence that "you [his brothers] intended to harm me, but God intended it for good to accomplish what is now being done, the saving of many lives" (Genesis 50:20). But it would take years for Joseph to understand that fully, and God's purposes could never be used to justify what the brothers did. What it proves is that grace has the power to change any situation.

So it would prove to be for Philemon and Onesimus. Even if we moderns might sympathise greatly with Onesimus wanting to run, it was still wrong and did not actually serve his best interests (especially if he got caught). After all, in the Colossians' household code, Paul instructed slaves to serve God within their servile status.

Yet accepting that God used this situation for good does not, paradoxically, mean we must assume divine approval for slavery. Quite the reverse in fact. See how subversive of the whole institution Paul is here. He wants Philemon to see his slave in a completely new light: no longer as a slave, but as a dear brother. That is radical—scandalous even. In fact, the terms in which Paul describes Onesimus are almost identical to those he has used for Philemon. There is no difference between them at all. Paul takes with utmost seriousness the radical equality that being justified by Christ brings. In Christ, there really is no slave or free (see Colossians 3:11). Philemon could hardly fail to notice the parallels in Paul's labels.

Just as Wedgwood's cameo appealed, is not Onesimus also a man and a brother? Despite everything Onesimus had done to let Philemon down, Paul dares to suggest that as a brother, he should be considered "even dearer" to Philemon now (Philemon **v 16**). People

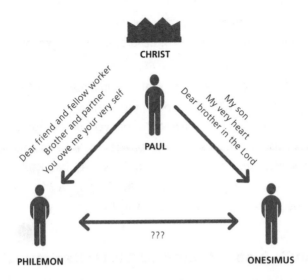

CHRIST

Dear friend and fellow worker
Brother and partner
You owe me your very self

My son
My very heart
Dear brother in the Lord

PAUL

PHILEMON

???

ONESIMUS

down the centuries have always struggled with such radical equality. We might not look down on slaves for the simple enough reason that we don't actually know any. But I can almost guarantee that you feel superior to some other class or group of people, regardless of the reasons for that. Setting ourselves up as superior to others is standard operating procedure for sinful people.

The Countess of Huntingdon (1707-1791) was another person who made a significant impact on eighteenth-century England. She was converted through George Whitefield's ministry, and became one of his most enthusiastic supporters. Whenever she could, she would invite members of her social circle to hear him. One was the Dowager Duchess of Buckingham and this was her reply to one such invitation:

"I thank your ladyship for the information concerning the Methodist preachers. Their doctrines are most repulsive and strongly tinctured with impertinence and disrespect before their superiors, in perpetually endeavouring to level all ranks and do away with all distinction. It is monstrous to be told you have a heart as sinful as the common wretches that crawl on the earth. This is highly offensive." (Arnold Dallimore, *George Whitefield*, *Volume 1*, page 132)

She was not wrong. It *is* offensive. But it doesn't make it untrue. We are all human. We are equally in need of grace, and equally receive grace through Christ.

But what exactly does Paul want to happen next to Onesimus? There has been much discussion about this, not least because he says that "you might have him back for ever" (**v 15**). He means at the very least that because of their conversions, slave and master are permanently bound to each other in Christ. Yet had Paul not just hinted at his desire to have Onesimus at his own side? Or does he in fact expect Onesimus to remain enslaved?

## 2. Paul's instructions and Christ-like ministry

Look carefully at Paul's instructions in **verses 17-22**. He has been clear what ought to happen (**v 8**). But each instruction has a nice twist back to something he has already written. The cumulative effect is nothing less than a depiction of a full reconciliation between master and slave, all in the light of the reconciliation brought about by Christ (Colossians 1:20).

- *Welcome Onesimus as if he were me* (Philemon **v 17**). There is a nice reversal here. Paul is saying that while he was in prison, One-simus had served him in Philemon's place. Now, he asks Philemon to welcome Onesimus's service in Paul's place. This is true part-nership, or *koinōnia*. This is how being bound together works.

- *Charge me what is owed* (**v 18**). If Onesimus had stolen from his master to aid his escape, then Paul wants to ensure that Philemon is not out of pocket. In fact, at this precise moment he stops dictating and signs an IOU in his own hand (**v 19**)! But there's another twist here. Just as Onesimus owes his conversion under God to Paul (**v 10**), so in fact does Philemon! With an **orator's** subtlety in mentioning what he says he won't mention, Philemon owes his "very self" (**v 19**)! Financial loss can no longer be an excuse for continued acrimony.

- *Refresh my heart* (**v 20**). Philemon has a well-deserved reputation for refreshing hearts (v 7). Paul now longs for his own share (**v 20**)! There is nice pun here, since the word translated "benefit" (*onaimeén*) is related to his new brother's name. This refreshing *onaimeén* will come through obediently welcoming Onesimus.

- *Get my room ready* (**v 22**). Paul expected to be released from jail in due course. He had various plans, including getting to Rome, Spain and perhaps beyond (see Romans 15:24). But in the meantime, coming to Colossae was another option. It was not to be, as far as we know. But Philemon had clearly been praying for Paul's release, and a visit would be an extra dimension to his answered prayer. Of course, a visit also meant that Paul could further assist in the reconciliation process if needed!

So what will happen now?

The ball is now in Philemon's court. The logic is obvious: Paul is Onesimus' father and brother in the Lord; Paul is Philemon's dear brother, and by implication, father in the Lord as well. Will Philemon draw the obvious conclusion? Will he be reconciled to Onesimus as his dear brother in Christ, and indeed "in" Paul?

Paul is confident of this reconciliation (Philemon **v 21**). The fact that this letter ended up in the New Testament suggests Paul was right to be. But was there more than reconciliation in Paul's mind? After all, he was sure that Philemon would "do even more than I ask". So could Onesimus' full emancipation be in view?

Paul never says so explicitly, but it is hard to imagine how Philemon and Onesimus could possibly have carried on as they were before. They were now family. Granting Onesimus his freedom would have been an obvious, if gracious, response. We have no way of verifying this, but the second bishop of Ephesus in the first century was called Onesimus. It was not a rare name, but it is not impossible that he was one and the same as Philemon's slave. Even if it was not him, it is entirely in keeping with the gospel revolution that a slave *could* become a bishop. He was clearly useful to Paul.

This letter, then, like the butterfly flapping its wings in one part of the world really did affect the rest of the world. Slavery could never be seen in the same light again—or at least, it should never have been once the letter had been properly understood. As Tom Wright comments:

> "But, like Jesus, his [Paul's] way of changing the world is to plant a grain of mustard seed, which, inconspicuous at first, grows into a spreading tree. And in the meantime … he teaches slaves and masters to treat themselves, and each other, as human beings. Like the artist or poet, he does some of his finest work not by the obscure clarity of direct statement, but by veiled allusion and teasing suggestion."
>
> (*Colossians and Philemon*, page 174)

As Paul bids farewell from his cell, alongside other friends who have featured in Colossians as well (**v 23-24**), he shares Christ's grace (**v 25**). For all the letter's subtlety and pastoral wisdom, the one thing that it is saturated with (in common with its sister letter to the Colossians) is grace. Onesimus did not deserve reconciliation; Philemon did not deserve Paul's paying off the losses that Onesimus had incurred. But this is what grace does—and some; because once begun, the tide of grace is unstoppable. And it changes the world.

It demands of us, at the very least, an examination of our own lives and communities for signs of "ungrace". Are there fellow believers with whom we refuse to be reconciled? Or be associated? Or share our lives? We may have every justification in avoiding them. We may have been grossly wronged. And of course, it can be very difficult if they don't acknowledge that there is something wrong, let alone accept responsibility for what they have done. This is where a third-party mediator is often necessary—as Paul was in this situation. But where there is truth, there can be reconciliation; if both sides are willing for it.

If not, then we have to ask what actual difference Christ's gospel makes for us.

No one said this was easy; but it is in the hardest circumstances—the acid test, if you like—that our faith in our grace-filled Rescuer, Christ, is proved to be genuine gold. It goes against every grain of our natures, but it is nothing less than the heart of the new self that we were clothed with when we came to know Christ for ourselves.

## Questions for reflection

1.  What can we learn from Paul's tact, humour, approach and style as he tries to reconcile these two brothers?

2.  Is there some deep division between members of your family or your church, in which you could act as a mediator? How might you approach the problem?

3.  How might you use this letter to answer the objections of someone who says that Christianity endorses slavery?

# GLOSSARY

**Abraham, Isaac and Jacob:** the "first fathers" or patriarchs of Israel, to whom God gave his promises.

**Apartheid:** a racist political system that treats whites and non-whites differently.

**Apostle:** one of the men appointed directly by the risen Christ to teach about him with authority.

**Arianism:** early Christian heresy that denied the divinity of Christ.

**Ascension:** when Jesus left earth to return to heaven, to sit and rule at God the Father's right hand (see Acts 1:6-11; Philippians 2:8-11).

**Blasphemy:** disrespecting or mocking God.

**Categorical:** a statement that is definite and explicit.

**Circumcision:** God told the men among his people in the Old Testament to be circumcised—have their foreskins cut off—as a way to show physically that they knew and trusted him, and belonged to the people of God (see Genesis 17).

**Conundrum:** a confusing and difficult problem or question.

**Convert:** someone who has changed from one religion to another.

**Coptic Christians:** members of an Egyptian church denomination.

**Covenant:** a binding agreement between two parties.

**Doctrine, Doctrinal:** statements of what is true about God.

**Euphoric:** a feeling of intense excitement and happiness.

**Evangelise, evangelism:** to tell non-Christians the gospel of Jesus Christ. An **evangelist** is a person who does this and equips other Christians to do it.

**Full-immersion baptism:** a form of baptism in which someone is completely submerged in water.

**Gentiles:** people who are not ethnically Jewish.

**Heresy:** a belief or opinion contrary to orthodox Christian doctrine taken from the Bible.

**Hindu:** adherent of an Indian religion that emphasizes freedom from the material world through purification of desires and elimination of personal identity. Hindu beliefs include reincarnation.

**Innocent third party:** someone who is not guilty of a crime, but who is drawn into the legal process and deemed to be guilty.

**Jehovah's Witnesses:** members of a heretical sect founded in the US by Charles Taze Russell (1852–1916). Jehovah's Witnesses deny many traditional Christian doctrines, including the trinity and the deity of Christ.

**John Wesley:** English evangelical minister and theologian (1703-1791) who founded Methodism.

**Joseph:** The second-youngest son of Jacob, and the great-grandson of Abraham. He was the first of Abraham's family to live in Egypt; the rest of the family followed him there, and in subsequent generations were enslaved.

**Kangaroo court:** an unofficial court held by a group of people in order to try someone regarded as guilty of a crime—usually without good evidence.

**Legalism:** a way of living that obeys certain rules in the belief that keeping these requirements will earn some form of blessing (for example, eternal life or worldly wealth).

**License:** living however you want to.

**Liturgy:** a form of public worship; the order and language of a church service.

**Martin Luther:** a German theologian in the sixteenth century during the Reformation. Luther taught that humans are made right with God through faith in Christ, not through what we do.

**Mediator:** someone who brings two enemies together and makes it possible for them to be friends again.

**Messiah:** God's promised, universal, eternal King—the Messiah, or Christ.

**Metaphor:** an image which is used to explain something, but which is not to be taken literally (e.g. "The news was a dagger to his heart").

**Metaphysics:** the study of abstract or spiritual concepts such as being, existence and reality. It often refers to things that cannot be measured physically.

**Methodist:** a member of the Methodist church: a free-church denomination founded by John Wesley.

**Monotheism:** the belief that there is only one God.

**Moral dilemma:** a conflict in which you have to choose between two or more actions and have moral reasons for choosing each action.

**Mormon:** a member of The Church of Jesus Christ of Latter-day Saints, a religion founded in the US in the 1820s by Joseph Smith Jr. Mormons are not trinitarian in their theology, and are not orthodox Christians.

**Moses:** the leader of God's people at the time when God brought them out of slavery in Egypt. God communicated his law (including the Ten Commandments) through Moses, and under his leadership guided them toward the land he had promised to give them.

**Muslim:** a follower of Islam.

**Mystical:** non-physical, spiritual.

**Orator:** an eloquent and skilled public speaker.

**Ordained:** someone who has been officially made a priest or minister by their church, usually by a higher church leader.

**Pagan:** someone who doesn't know and worship the true God.

**Paradox:** two true statements that seem to be contradictory, but aren't.

**Pharisee:** leaders of a first-century Jewish sect who were extremely strict about keeping God's laws externally, and who added extra laws around God's law, to ensure that they wouldn't break it.

**Platitude:** a phrase that is so over-used that it has come to lack any real meaning.

**Psalmist:** poet or musician who wrote one of the psalms.

**Purgatory:** in Roman Catholic thought, the place where the souls of the dead are believed to go to be "purged" of their sin, before they are fit to enter heaven.

**Puritans:** a member of a sixteenth- and seventeenth-century movement in Great Britain which was committed to the Bible as God's word, to simpler worship services, to greater commitment and devotion to following Christ, and increasingly to resisting the institutional church's hierarchical structures. Many emigrated to what would become the US, and were a strong influence on the church in most of the early colonies.

**Rabbi:** a Jewish religious teacher.

**Reformation:** a sixteenth-century movement for the reform of abuses in the Roman Catholic Church which resulted in the establishment of the Protestant Churches.

**Relative:** here, a statement that is in relation or in proportion to something else.

**Scythian:** a member of a warrior tribe of nomads from southern Russia in ancient times.

**Second Coming:** referring to the prophesied return of Christ to earth at the last judgment.

**Sect:** small religious group that has separated from the main religion.

**Shalom:** Hebrew word often translated "peace". It's full meaning involves ideas of fruitful flourishing.

**Sovereign:** to have supreme authority / be the supreme ruler.

**Sway:** under the control or influence of someone or something.

**Sycophantic:** praising people in authority in a way that is not sincere, usually in order to get some advantage from them.

**Synagogues:** local places of worship, prayer and teaching for Jewish people.

**Systematic Theology:** teaching about God and the Bible that is arranged by doctrines in a consistent way.

**Tabernacle:** a large, tented area where the Israelites worshipped God, and where his presence symbolically dwelled (see Exodus 26; 40).

**Tenses:** the form a verb takes to show *when* something happened. There are three main tenses—past, present and future—but many other variations on them.

**Theology:** the study of what is true about God.

**Tithe:** referring to the Old Testament command to give a tenth of someone's crops to God.

**Totalitarian:** a system of government that requires complete submission to the state in every area of life.

**Unitarian:** someone who asserts the unity of God and rejects the doctrine of the Trinity.

**Universal:** something that is applicable to all people and things in the world.

**Virtuous circle:** a recurring cycle of events, the result of each one being to increase the beneficial effect of the next.

**Worldview:** the beliefs we hold in an attempt to make sense of the world as we experience it, and which direct how we live in it. Everyone has a worldview.

# BIBLIOGRAPHY

- Michael Card, *A Better Freedom: Finding Life as Slaves of Christ* (IVP, 2009). A very helpful overview of the theme of slavery in the Bible, especially sensitive in the light of the Transatlantic Slave Trade.

- Arnold Dallimore, *George Whitefield: The Life and Times of the Great Evangelist of the 18th Century Revival, Volume 1* (Banner of Truth, 1970).

- Os Guinness, *Time for Truth* (IVP, 2000).

- Al Hsu, *The Single Issue* (IVP, 1998).

- Aldous Huxley, *Ends and Means* (Chatto & Windus, 1946).

- Timothy Keller, *The Reason for God* (Dutton, 2008).

- C.S. Lewis, *Mere Christianity* (William Collins, 2016).

- R.C. Lucas, *Fullness & Freedom: The Message of Colossians & Philemon* in The Bible Speaks Today Series (IVP, 1980). Still relevant and helpful for getting the flow of the letters.

- E McLuhan and F. Zingrone (Editors), *Essential McLuhan* (BasicBooks, 1995).

- Mark Meynell, *The New Testament and Slavery: Approaches and Implications* (Latimer Trust 2007). A published version of my Masters thesis.

- D.J. Moo, *The Letters to the Colossians and to Philemon* in the Pillar New Testament Commentary Series (Eerdmans, 2008). This is my main go-to commentary for in-depth study.

- John Pollock, *Shaftesbury: The Poor Man's Earl* (Hodder & Stoughton, 1986).

- Richard Sibbes, *Light from Heaven* (Sovereign Grace Publishers, 2001).

- John Stott, *The Incomparable Christ* (IVP, 2001). A brilliant overview of the Bible's teaching about Jesus, with very helpful sections on his universal lordship.

- Joni Eareckson Tada, *The God I Love: A Lifetime of Walking with Jesus* (Zondervan, 2003).

- Stan Telchin, *Abandoned* (Marshall Pickering, 1998).

- Robert Wall, *Colossians & Philemon* in the IVP New Testament Commentary Series (IVP, 1993).

- Brian Walsh and Sylvia Keesmaat, *Colossians Remixed: Subverting the Empire* (IVP USA, 2004). Quirky, sometimes infuriating, often subversive, but always stimulating.

- Walter Wink, *Naming the Powers: The Language of Power in the New Testament* (Fortress Press, 1984).

- N.T. Wright, *Colossians and Philemon* in the Tyndale New Testament Commentary Series (IVP, 1986). Good for a basic introduction to the main interpretation questions.

# Colossians for...
## Bible-study Groups

Mark Meynell's **Good Book Guide** to Colossians is the companion to this resource, helping groups of Christians to explore, discuss and apply the book together. Six studies—each including Investigation, Apply, Getting Personal, Pray, and Explore More sections—take you through the whole of Colossians. It includes a concise Leader's Guide at the back.

Find out more at:
**www.thegoodbook.com/goodbookguides**

# Daily Devotionals

***Explore*** daily devotional helps you open up the Scriptures and will encourage and equip you in your walk with God. Available as a quarterly booklet, *Explore* is also available as an app, where you can download notes on Colossians, alongside contributions from trusted Bible teachers including Timothy Keller, Mark Dever, Tim Chester, Albert Mohler, Jr., and Sam Allberry.

Find out more at:
**www.thegoodbook.com/explore**

# More For You

## Galatians For You

"The book of Galatians is dynamite. It is an explosion of joy and freedom which leaves us enjoying a life of blessing. I pray that it explodes in your heart as you read this book."

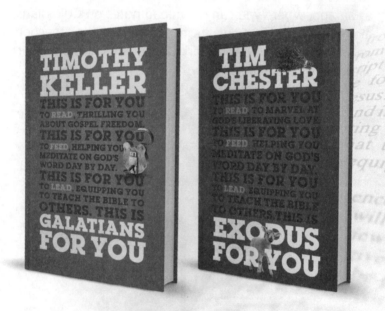

## Exodus For You

"Exodus is key to understanding Jesus. It is an exciting story, a historical story and—as it points us to and inspires us to worship Jesus—it is *our* story."

# The Series

Other titles in the *God's Word For You* series are:

- **Exodus For You** Tim Chester
- **Judges For You** Timothy Keller
- **1 Samuel For You** Tim Chester
- **2 Samuel For You** Tim Chester
- **Daniel For You** David Helm
- **Micah For You** Stephen Um
- **Luke 1-12 For You** Mike McKinley
- **Luke 12-24 For You** Mike McKinley
- **John 1-12 For You** Josh Moody
- **Acts 1-12 For You** Albert Mohler, Jr.
- **Romans 1-7 For You** Timothy Keller
- **Romans 8-16 For You** Timothy Keller
- **Galatians For You** Timothy Keller
- **Ephesians For You** Richard Coekin
- **Philippians For You** Steven Lawson
- **Titus For You** Tim Chester
- **James For You** Sam Allberry
- **1 Peter For You** Juan Sanchez

Find out more about these resources, and news about upcoming titles in the series, at:

**www.thegoodbook.com/for-you**

# Good Book Guides
## for groups and individuals

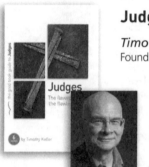

### Judges: The flawed and the flawless

*Timothy Keller*
Founding Pastor, Redeemer Presbyterian Church, Manhattan

Welcome to a time when God's people were deeply flawed, often failing, and struggling to live in a world which worshipped other gods. Our world is not so different—we need Judges to equip us to live for God in our day, and remind us that he is a God of patience and mercy.
*Also by Tim Keller: Romans 1–7; Romans 8–16; Galatians*

### Daniel: Staying strong in a hostile world

*David Helm*
Lead Pastor, Holy Trinity Church, Chicago

The first half of Daniel is well known and much loved. The second is little read and less understood. David Helm leads groups through the whole book, showing how the truths about God in the second half enabled Daniel and his friends—and will inspire us—to live faithful, courageous lives.

### Esther: Royal rescue

*Jane McNabb*
Chair of the London Women's Convention

The experience of God's people in Esther's day helps us in those moments when we question God's sovereignty, his love, or his faithfulness. Their story reveals that despite appearances, God is in control, and he answers his people's prayers—often in most unexpected ways.